Closer to God

Closer to God

Practical help
on your spiritual journey

EDITED BY IAN BUNTING

SCRIPTURE UNION
130 CITY ROAD LONDON EC1V 2NJ

Cover illustration by Rosemary Woods.

Cover design by Mark Carpenter Design Consultants.

Phototypeset by Intype, London.

Printed and bound in Great Britain by Cox and Wyman Ltd, Reading.

CONTENTS

ACKNOWLEDGEMENTS

Page 19: Henri Nouwen, from *The Genesee Diary (Report from a Trappist Monastery)*, Doubleday 1981.

Page 22: Gerard Hughes, from *God of Surprises*, Darton, Longman & Todd Ltd, London 1985.

Page 35: Collect for All Saints' Day, from *The Alternative Service Book*. Copyright © The Central Board of the Finance of the Church of England 1980.

Page 36: Statement on Baptism, from *Baptism, Eucharist and Ministry*, pp 2–3. Copyright © 1982 WCC Publications, World Council of Churches, Geneva, Switzerland. Thomas Ashe, from *Morning, Noon and Night*, ed. John Carden, Church Missionary Society (CMS) 1976.

Page 39: Collect for the last Sunday after Pentecost, from *The Alternative Service Book*. Copyright © The Central Board of the Finance of the Church of England 1980.

Page 42: Eugene Peterson, from *Working the Angles*, Eerdmans 1987.

Pages 43, 51: Samuel Escobar, from 'The Hermeneutical Task in Global Economics', *Transformation*, Vol 3/4, Jun–Dec 1987, p 7ff. OCMS, Box 70, Oxford – an international evangelical dialogue on mission and ethics.

Page 56, 179/80: Dietrich Bonhoeffer, from *Life Together*, SCM Press Ltd. Permission sought.

Page 62: Margaret Hebblethwaite, from *Finding God in All Things: Praying with St Ignatius*, Fount 1987.

Page 73: The Grail Prayer. By permission of The Grail (England).

Page 84/5: Garrison Keillor, from *Lake Wobegon Days*, Faber & Faber 1986.

Page 94: Rosalind Rinker, taken from the book, *Prayer: Conversing with God* by Rosalind Rinker. Copyright © 1970 by Zondervan Publishing House. Used by permission of Zondervan Publishing House.

Page 129: Karol, from *Dare to Live*, SPCK (Les presses de Taizé) 1974. Permission sought.

Page 162: Simon Tugwell, from 'Living with God', *Prayer* Vol 1, Veritas, Dublin 1974.

Page 171: Carlos Mesters, from *Deus, Onde Estas? Curso de Biblia*, Belo Horizonte, Vega 1971, 1–3.

Page 197: Simon Tugwell, from 'Prayer in Practice', *Prayer* Vol 2, Veritas, Dublin 1974.

Page 198: Dietrich Bonhoeffer, from *Cost of Discipleship*, SCM Press Ltd 1964. Permission sought.

Page 200: Paul Tournier, from *A Doctor's Casebook in the Light of the Bible*, SCM Press 1969.

Pages 212, 217/8 and 219: Permission sought for extracts by Chester P Michael and Marie C Norrisey, Olive Wyon, and John Welch.

1

GETTING STARTED

Ian Bunting

We come to God because we believe God is. God made us. God loves us and we can know God. When we take up a book like this, therefore, it is a sign of hope. We want to get to know God better. This is not a hopeless quest. God has given us signposts and markers along the way. We find them in the world about us (Psalm 19:1). We discover them in our own soul-searching (Psalm 139:13–16). History and, above all, the Bible point us in the right direction (Psalm 119:105). Central to the history of God's dealings with people is the story of Jesus Christ. We can become part of that ongoing story of God's work through Jesus Christ and be led along the same path that his disciples followed. They travelled, and we travel, in the power of God's Spirit.

WE ARE ALL DIFFERENT

Christians are all different. It seems an obvious thing to say but we sometimes create problems for ourselves, and others, when we forget it. We are tempted to feel that we, or they, must conform to some pattern. If we don't, then we feel that we have failed. Yet we have all been made differently. For example, some of us rely on our feelings; others are practical; some are achievement oriented; and others put the emphasis on thinking. Probably we all have elements of these characteristics, but the chances are that we lean in one direction more than another.

Some who read this book will set great store by their feelings. One could call them 'Mary' Christians. Mary stands out in the Bible as one who was deeply moved by her relationship with Jesus, for example when she anointed his feet and wiped them with her hair (John 12:3). For readers who share her temperament, it will be important to feel loved by God and to love God in return. To be a Christian is to enter into a love-relationship with Jesus Christ, much as two people share a love-relationship in friendship or marriage. As time goes by, if the relationship is strong, it deepens to the point where early expressions of passionate feeling give way to an intuition that you love and are loved. Maybe the relationship even grows to the stage where neither words nor signs are needed to express it. You know and love Jesus, and he loves you, and that is all that matters.

Another reader will be much more matter-of-fact about believing in God and following Christ. If Christianity is to mean anything, it must work. Things must change. *I* must change. One could call such a disciple a 'Peter' Christian. However, Peter was always spoiling his discipleship. He wanted to walk on water (Matthew 14:28); he wanted to be faithful to Jesus and, if necessary, even to die with him (Matthew 26:35); but he kept on slipping up. Nevertheless, Peter wanted to change and he was changed. The time came when he did miracles like Jesus (Acts 3:6), was faithful when challenged (Acts 5:29) and, according to tradition, died for his faith. The Christian who is like Peter is probably looking for personal change. What we know in ourselves to be bad begins – we hope – to be replaced by what we know to be good. A sure sign of progress is when some of the selfishness in us gives way to evidence of the growing fruit of the Spirit (Galatians 5:16–26).

Other Christians will be achievement-oriented, go-getting. They see targets and aim to reach them. They are 'Paul' Christians. Paul knew what he wanted and, having identified his goal of being united to Christ in his ongoing mission, he was committed to achieving it (Philippians 3:14). Such Christians want to have a clear sense of purpose in their lives. They concentrate especially, perhaps, on seeing relatives and friends converted, on bringing up a Christian family, on serving overseas or on keeping the faith, like Paul, to their dying day.

Thinking disciples are 'John' Christians. John looked for a faith which can be understood and owned by those who believe. The whole purpose of his writing was that his friends might know, and be assured of, their faith in Christ (1 John 5:13). These Christians realise that the way we think is closely related to the way we behave: 'Be careful how you think; your life is shaped by your thoughts' (Proverbs 4:23, GNB).

There is a sense, as we noted, in which we are all feeling, practical, achieving and thinking Christians. We are likely to respond more readily, however, when the message we hear challenges or stimulates us along the lines of one of our personality traits. It is good to become aware of the sort of people we are. This is not because we want to be unresponsive to other kinds of messages, but because we want to recognise the particular and unique way in which God speaks to each one of us according to the different personalities which he has made and given to us.

DISCIPLESHIP

The first Christians got their name because they followed Jesus *Christ* (Acts 11:26). This means that, though we are different from each other, we are all travelling along the same road, the one which Jesus has travelled ahead of us. However, we never travel, at least on this earth, as far as our Master has gone before us. Like the Israelites who crossed the Jordan, we have never been this way before. Each step of the road is new. This is why experienced Christians remind us that to be a disciple of Jesus means taking one step at a time, as we continue walking and learning day by day.

> Lord Jesus Christ, we thank you for all the benefits you have won for us, for all the pains and insults you have borne for us. Most merciful redeemer, friend and brother, may we know you more clearly, love you more dearly and follow you more nearly, day by day. Amen.   *St Richard of Chichester*

Although the lesson is obvious, Christians are still prone to getting stuck. We travel so far along the road and then we stop. It makes no sense but it happens. Sometimes we stop because we get tired. When we first believed in Jesus, the road ahead seemed full of promise. Then it became hard and rough. Maybe, like Demas, who loved the life of this world too much (2 Timothy 4:10), we found it hard to keep going in the Jesus way. Sometimes we stop because we think we have arrived. We think we have become the kind of people Jesus expects his disciples to be. Maybe we have enjoyed the spiritual gifts which God has given us and, although we would never admit it, we behave as though there is nothing more to be learnt. The consequence of such presumption is disaster (1 Corinthians 10:12). There is always more to love, more to grow, more to achieve and more to know.

The Christian road is *not* an easy one. This is why in the New Testament discipleship is sometimes also talked about as a struggle. It *is* a struggle with ourselves because we often find that we want to become, and to accomplish, more than it is within our power to accomplish. Paul recognised this problem in himself and felt the profound disappointment which comes when we fail to keep our own standards, let alone God's (Romans 7:19–25).

> In this life, there are two loves fighting each other in every temptation: love of God and love of the world, and whichever wins draws its lover in its train as by a weight. *St Augustine*

Christians also find themselves engaged with an enemy outside themselves. Sometimes Christians feel oppressed by the power of evil (Romans 7:21). At other times it seems as though we struggle with evil, non-human powers (Ephesians 6:12). In the midst of this, it is easy to be overwhelmed by fear or hopelessness and to feel like giving up the battle.

The Bible assures us that we are not 'orphans' (John 14:18). Jesus promises that God will come to his disciples and make a home with them (John 14:23). When we grasp the way that God – the Father, Son and the Spirit – accompanies us, the picture changes. No longer do we see ourselves as travelling alone without hope and struggling in despair. Instead, we become pilgrims with a clear destination and a travelling companion. We are soldiers with victory in sight and our commander alongside. And, even more promising, we are new beings in Christ. The old has gone, the new has come (2 Corinthians 5:17). With God making a home in us, our view of the world changes. We begin to see with the eyes of God, to look at life from his perspective.

WHICH WAY?

We have been describing a journey of discovery about ourselves, about God, about the world and about each other. Every traveller is grateful for maps and guides which tell of what others have found. They suggest the best and most reliable routes to take. The Bible is the best guide of all and gives the Christian a handbook for every day living which reflects everybody's joys, sorrows and temptations. We need to remember it is not just a history book. It is a journey planner for those who want to move into unexplored territory. It could be that you want to get moving again after a period of standing still. Someone else, perhaps, wants to try a different path in order to get nearer God and to get to know God better. John Newton said:

> If you want to love Him better now while you are here . . . trust Him. The more you trust Him, the better you will love Him. If you ask farther, How shall I do to trust Him? I answer, Try Him. The more you make trial of Him, the more your trust in Him will be strengthened.

Christianity is an *experimental* religion, for people who want to try God out. Being a Christian is about discovering truth through believing God and following Jesus' teaching.

> Jesus answered, 'My teaching is not my own. It comes from him who sent me. If anyone chooses to do God's will, he will find out whether my teaching comes from God or whether I speak on my own.'   *John 7:16–17*

This book offers suggestions for those who want to live closer to God. For instance, if you are a 'Mary' Christian, with a big dependence on how you feel as an indicator of where you stand in relation to God, there are many ideas which may help you along the lines of your God-given personality. You may find it stimulating to experiment with the use of your senses in prayer, or to use bodily movements to express praise, penitence, worship and commitment as you approach God. For someone further along the road, a creative entry into silence may open a new vista on the depths of God's love.

The practical 'Peter' Christian may find it helpful to join a prayer group in which there is honest sharing. Or it may be helpful to start a spiritual journal as a way of building into your life a periodic spiritual check-up on your growth as a disciple. Further on? A spiritual director could serve as an inspiring personal consultant.

The achieving 'Paul' Christian may benefit from a new and, perhaps, unfamiliar spiritual challenge. It could be to tithe your income for the first time, or to fast and pray for a particular miracle you believe God wants to perform. It might involve taking a fresh look at one's political understanding and beliefs with a determination to set some goals and begin working towards them.

The reflective 'John' Christian may well love to read Christian books. However, many modern Christians have yet to discover the treasures of the past. Some of the quotations in this book send us back to learn again the lessons of believers who come from another age, a different culture, and who found, in some cases, strange (to us) ways of getting to know God better. Yet their experiences can help us along our own paths of discovery today.

It is important to remember that we can all learn from practices and insights which may, at first, seem unappealing or even threatening. It could be that, in the same way that jogging is good for the unfit, a spiritual discipline which threatens us could be just what we need. In fact, just as the people of the Western world are too comfortable in terms of wealth, possessions and leisure – at least in relation to the developing world – so Christians easily fall prey to a comfortable Christianity which makes few demands and certainly does not lead to spiritual maturity. This book challenges its readers to exercise greater spiritual discipline, and gives some clues as to how to go about it.

BETTER TOGETHER

A mistake often made is to think that Christian discipleship is a matter of individual devotion and discipline. Certainly there are some Christians who are by nature introverted. They prefer to be on their own, so they tend to grow in their Christian lives through private meditation and prayer, and often they experience an inner life which is strong, full of colour and meaning. It is not that they do not like people, Christian fellowship or participating in church services; it is just that they prefer more solitary ways of growing closer to God.

However, such Christians need to remember that, whether or not we like to spend time with our brothers and sisters in Christ, we are never Christians on our own. Ours is not a private religion. We are not our own masters and judges. We live in a whole network and we belong to each other as we follow Christ together. That is why the second chapter of this book is about our worship and life together as Christians. To be sure, some of us are more gregarious than others but, whether we like it or not, we are bonded together as the people of God (1 Peter 2:9–10) and the body of Christ (1 Corinthians 12:27). We are the community of faith. We express it in worship, in our Christian celebrations, in our music, in our social gatherings, as well as in our small group gatherings for study, prayer and fellowship. Consequently, we hope that some will also use this book as a resource for group study and sharing.

EXPECT SURPRISES!

Great Christians from the past have an important part to play in giving depth to our discipleship. We are often in bondage to modernity and it is easy to forget the debt of gratitude we owe to the saints in heaven with whom we not only share our worship but who have left us their example and teaching: 'Remember your leaders, who spoke the word of God to you. Consider the outcome of their way of life and imitate their faith' (Hebrews 13:7).

This book is illustrated with some of the pithy sayings, poetry, practices, prayers and examples of Christians who are now in glory, but who have left us a rich inheritance. Some of the ancient ways are strange to a generation which seeks immediate access, gratification or success. For example, life-long devotion, skill and insight go into the making and use of an icon. It is too facile to dismiss automatically the use of an icon as superstition. A retreat, particularly a silent one, may seem a terrible waste of time to an activist Christian who is not ready to consider, for example, how important it could be to stop and recharge the batteries in order to be more effective and less prone to breakdown. Again, fasting might seem totally impractical: it is not as though my abstinence will help to feed the hungry and it could make me tired, irritable and lethargic. Yet this important spiritual discipline is an effective means of concentrating the mind and sharpening the spiritual perception of the believer.

A few readers may feel anxious about some of the suggestions in this book. For although all the contributors relate easily and naturally to, and have been nurtured in, the traditional disciplines of evangelical spirituality, we have also come to appreciate the way Christians from other countries and traditions have discovered their own ways of living closer to God. We have been willing to explore from other traditions any insights into the development of the spiritual life which accord with the Bible's teaching, and we encourage other Christians to do the same. For example, we associate the stations of the Cross with Catholic Christendom, and may think of them as having to do with an externally imposed 'penance' rather than the devotional aid they can be. Yet to observe them may help us to a much deeper perception of the event which lies at the heart of our faith – the death and resurrection of our Lord Jesus Christ. A biblical parallel of this kind can be seen in the institution of the Passover which is a visual reminder detailing the Jews' practical experience of God's salvation. Often we associate the crucifixion and resurrection more with our Christian beginnings than, as Paul did, with our Christian living day by day (1 Corinthians 1:23–25 and especially Philippians 3:10). We need all the help we can get to do both.

BEGINNINGS

There is no 'right' way to go through this handbook. If you are the kind of person who likes to go through a book from cover to cover, so be it. But this book was not written or intended to be used in that way. You could start with a section that looks stimulating. Or you could begin with what looks unfamiliar and threatening. Often it is when we are confronted by new experiences and new adventures with God, that we grow as Christians, travel further and win more ground. That said, self-criticism, not necessarily all negative, and repentance are good places for us all to begin.

Try out the following two checklists: the first is an exercise in self-awareness; the second, an exercise in sensitivity to others.

Self-awareness
1   What is your relationship with God now?
2   What changes, for better or worse, can you detect in your life during the last year?
3   What goals in your life have you achieved or failed to achieve?
4   In what way do you think your knowledge of God has grown?
5   In what ways or areas of your life are you aware of resisting God?
6   What habits are inhibiting you from going further?
7   Which spiritual enemies are hindering or attacking you now?
8   Are you self-disciplined in the areas of food, sleep, fitness and leisure activity?
9   Do the books, magazines and papers you read tend to broaden or narrow your horizons?
10   What are your biggest fears and hopes?
11   What opinion do you have of yourself right now?
12   What will you pray for as you work through this book?

The chances are that we will be disappointed as we answer these questions, but it is important to remember that this is no reason to hate ourselves as human beings. That would be to misread the nature of God who loves us and who has assured us that we are of infinite value to him by sending his Son, Jesus Christ, to die for us. As we answer the questions honestly, we become aware, however, of two very significant aspects of the sin of humankind. It is not only our personal, specific shortcomings which offend against God's love, it is our rebellious heart, mind and will which set themselves against him. In short, sin is much more than personal failure, it is the offence of a fundamentally anti-God nature. And we do not sin against God alone because, as we have seen, we are not only individuals but human beings caught up in a whole network of relationships; therefore, we find that we sin against our neighbour too. Here, then, is the second checklist.

Sensitivity to others

1 How good are your relationships with your spouse (if you are married) and friends?
2 In what ways are your friendships growing or shrinking?
3 Have your efforts to achieve your personal goals affected your relationships with your spouse or friends?
4 How highly do you rate the contribution of others as you try to get to know God better?
5 What are the outstanding and unresolved conflicts with other people in your life?
6 How well are you coping with your sexual desires at present?
7 Are your friendships with unbelievers rich and rewarding?
8 As you continue to pray for others, how do you hope this book will help you in your relationships with them?

REPENTANCE

So long as you have not reached the realm of tears, that which is within you still serves the world – that is, you still lead a worldly life and do the work of God only with your outer man, while the inner man is barren; for his fruit begins with tears.

Isaac of Nineveh

We have been thinking of the Christian life as a journey and a struggle; but the basis of it, the point from which it takes its origin, is a change of citizenship. We become citizens of the kingdom of God. The change is a radical one, and not only do we have new privileges and new responsibilities, we have a new identity. This fundamental change can be compared to being adopted into a new family.

However, we have a problem. We fail in the duties of our citizenship; we are irresponsible family members. So dealing with sin is not just part of becoming a Christian, it is part of being a Christian. The solution of the problem lies in the death of Christ. We reach the solution by standing, as it were, at the foot of the cross. But how do we get to that point? Sometimes we feel paralysed by sin and seem unable to change. Sometimes we do not know how to respond to God. Repentance – the process of having our sins dealt with – can be thought of as a series of steps.

Recognise the sin

First of all, we need to recognise what the sin is, to identify and name it – not the problem, or something near to the sin, or a result of the sin, but what the sin is. What have I done – in thought, word or deed – which can be described as a sin against God? After all, you can't repent of something until you have actually recognised what it is.

For example, consider a man who wants to talk with God about his relationship with his wife. It is not helpful for him to say, 'Lord, I want to confess to you that my relationship with my wife is not very good.' This man needs to name some precise things that he is doing that contribute to the breakdown of the relationship. Maybe he needs to confess, 'Lord, I don't listen very closely when she is talking to me – but he needs to be specific.

Repent of the sin

To repent means to turn from sin to God. So we need to look

at the past – that sin we have named – and see it as God sees it. If we can imagine Jesus being with us in that past event, we will begin to feel that deep regret over sin which is the start of repentance. The man whose situation we have been considering might need to say to God, 'I thought it didn't affect my relationship with my wife, but now I see that it was a sign of selfishness and was hurtful. I am sorry and I don't want to be like that in future.'

Receive God's forgiveness

We need to receive God's forgiveness for specific sins. Stop and say, 'I now receive your forgiveness for this particular sin', and name the sin. God's word promises forgiveness: 'If we confess our sins, he is faithful and just and will forgive us our sins and purify us from all unrighteousness' (1 John 1:9). You may find that a physical act such as unclenching your fist, to symbolise your repentance, and spreading your open hands palm up, to symbolise your receiving of God's forgiveness, can help. Even breathing (breathe out as a sign of giving a sin to God, and in as a sign of receiving God's forgiveness) can help us to know deep down that not only has God offered forgiveness, but we have received it.

Look to the future

Repentance means turning from sin to God, so we need to think about the future. If we are contrite over past sins, we should determine to be different next time: 'Next time my wife wants to tell me about her day when I get in from work, I will put down the paper and turn off the television so that I'm not distracted from listening to what it is important for her to say to me'. This exercise of will is what makes repentance comparable to a change of direction: we are going to stop going in the wrong direction and start to live God's way.

Ask for help

Finally, we should ask for the help of the Holy Spirit. We need the Spirit's help throughout the Christian life, but never more so than when we are struggling to leave sin behind and live God's way.

Now you're ready to 'try out' the first seven days' exercises provided here. They aim to help you think about what you are like, where you are and where you want to go. Enjoy your journey!

TAKE SEVEN DAYS ...

Day 1 Especially for those to whom feelings matter most

• Imagine yourself standing by a fast-flowing river. In the middle of the white water there is a rock. Think about the rock. It is well-grounded and doesn't move as the water rushes past. Now, in your imagination, stand on that rock. What does it feel like?

• Read Psalm 42 while, in your imagination, you still stand on the rock.

How do you feel about the fears and the longings of the writer of the psalm?

Look out for all the reliable qualities of God which are mentioned.

Talk to God in the same way as the psalmist and thank him where you can.

Is there a quiet stream underneath the fluctuating affirmations and rejections of my little world? Is there a still point where my life is anchored and from which I can reach out with hope and courage and confidence?
Henri Nouwen

Day 2 Especially for the practical Christian

• List on a piece of paper three changes which you would like to see:

in your own life
in your relationships with others
in their relationships with you

What prevents these changes taking place? What course of

action will you take to overcome the problems?

• Read Galatians 5:16–26. Note especially verses 16, 18 and 25. They remind us that, at the end of the day, the change must come from God, though not without our co-operation. The key to success lies in the work of God's Spirit. We cannot change by ourselves.

• Learn by heart Galatians 2:20: 'I no longer live, but Christ lives in me. The life I live in the body, I live by faith in the Son of God, who loved me and gave himself for me.'

Day 3 Especially for the Christian achiever

• Spend a few moments reviewing your ambitions.

What is really important for you in life?
What motivates you as a Christian – in your family, in your work, in the world, at church?

• Read Philippians 1:12–26. What was the secret of Paul's single-minded determination to preach the gospel? How did Paul regard his difficult circumstances?

• Learn Philippians 4:13. Go over, in your mind, all the engagements for today. To what are you looking forward, and what do you dread? Say the verse to yourself during the day, every time you move from one activity to the next. It will help you to face any challenges you are tempted to avoid. 'I can do everything through him who gives me strength.'

Day 4 Especially for the Christian in search of understanding

> I fled Him, down the nights and down the days;
> I fled Him, down the arches of the years;
> I fled Him, down the labyrinthine ways
> Of my own mind; and in the midst of tears
> I hid from Him, and under running laughter.
> Up vistaed hopes I sped
> And shot, precipitated,
> Adown Titanic glooms of chasmèd fears.
> From those strong Feet that followed, followed after.

But with unhurrying chase,
And unperturbèd pace,
Deliberate speed, majestic instancy,
They beat – and a Voice beat
More instant than the Feet –
'All things betray thee, who betrayest Me.'

. . . Halts by me that footfall:
Is my gloom, after all,
Shade of His hand, outstretched caressingly?
'Ah, fondest, blindest, weakest,
I am He Whom thou seekest!
Thou dravest love from thee, who dravest Me.'

Francis Thompson, 1859–1907
(from *The Hound of Heaven*)

• Do you also find that God is inescapable? Read Psalm 139:1–18.

• Try to recapture one of your recurring nightmares (if you have them), for example, an attempt to escape some kind of pursuer. It is a relief to wake up and discover that we are in the real world where we know, however inadequate we may be, that God loves us. 'When I awake, I am still with you' (Psalm 139:18).

Alternatively, go over some of the significant moments of your life from your earliest days. Are you able to understand how the writer of the psalm interprets God's hand in every stage? Turn each thought into a prayer of thanksgiving.

You may not hear him coming after you, but you will know it when he has hold of you.

George MacDonald

Day 5 An exercise for a traveller

• Think of your life as a journey home from work.

What sort of day has it been?
How do you feel?
Did anything change?

Was anything achieved?
Do you see anything in a different light?

• Read Luke 24:13–35. Imagine that you are joining the two disciples on the road to Emmaus.

What are they saying about their day in Jerusalem?
How are they describing it to you?
What difference does it make when Jesus joins them on the journey?
Does Jesus help you to see your day in a new light?
Are you able to recognise the signs that he is with you?
Can he help you come to a different judgement on the day's events?

> I want to know Christ and the power of his resurrection and the fellowship of sharing in his sufferings, becoming like him in his death, and so, somehow, to attain to the resurrection from the dead.
>
> *Philippians 3:10–11*

Day 6 For the Christian soldier

• When people are angry, they sometimes do uncharacteristic things. They may drive too fast, or pick quarrels with others. Perhaps you just burn inwardly with resentment. What is it that makes you angry?

> Most of our suffering comes to us not because our lives are dedicated to promoting Christ's kingdom but from frustration at our failure to build our own kingdom of wealth, honour and power, from knowledge of our own incompetence, feelings of inferiority, from physical weakness or mental slowness, from difficulties of temperament, loneliness, inability to love or be loved, in which there is no glory, no heroism, just a pathetic mediocrity. *Gerard Hughes*

• Read Ephesians 6:10–18. The armour of God protects us from despair about ourselves. It also equips us for battle with the enemies of God.

• What are some of the things which make God angry? Do we feel the same way about them? Some people avoid what they cannot face. Some people face what they cannot avoid. God wants us to engage with the powers that oppose his kingdom whether or not we can avoid them.

Day 7 A reminder of our togetherness

• Make a point of meeting with another Christian today. What place and function does that Christian have within the body of Christ?

• Read 1 Corinthians 12:12–27. Paul emphasises the important part played by the weaker member of Christ's body (v 22). Everyone is dependent upon everyone else (v 25). The body relies for its effective working upon the participation and mutually responsible action of each of its parts (v 27).

• Think of the Christian you have met today and ask yourself:

What has this Christian to give me?
What gift have I to share with him or her?
Is there someone we can help, or something we can do, together?
If the Christian in question is *not* my friend, why not?

• Sometimes it needs a group of people to come together to enable change to take place. Together with other Christians, you could talk about the following:

What needs changing in our community, in our office, in our nation?
Is it possible to bring together a group of people with a common concern and work out ways of achieving the changes we have identified as being necessary?

2

PRAYING WITH THE CHURCH

Michael Vasey

When Jesus was asked by his disciples how they should pray, he replied by teaching them a prayer (Luke 11:1–4). It is a prayer that has been found on the lips of Christians ever since. Christians have learnt it in childhood and have prayed it on their death-bed or in moments of deep distress and confusion. The simple words have brought men and women of many cultures into the presence of God. Over many centuries its short petitions have taught Christians to set their hope on the changes that God will bring. The range of human concerns are to be found in this prayer: physical need, human wrongdoing, failed human relationships, and confrontation with the mystery of evil. The prayer's name for God brings immediate comfort. At the same time it stretches the greatest minds among the church's thinkers as they try to fathom how we are admitted into Jesus' relationship with one 'whom no one has seen or can see' (1 Timothy 6:16) but whom Jesus called 'Father'.

NOT ALONE
When we pray the Lord's Prayer, we enter the infinite sea of the church's prayer life. Two phrases in the prayer show that Christians neither live nor pray alone. 'As we forgive those who sin against us' prevents us ever thinking that Christian prayer can be an escape from life with others; it is engagement with life even at its most hurtful. 'Our Father' introduces us

to a deeper mystery. Even when you 'go into your room, close the door and pray to your Father ... who sees what is done in secret' (Matthew 6:6), your life is intimately bound up with those who are in Christ with you.

One or many?

Each individual is infinitely precious to God. Jesus fulfils his own story of the shepherd who leaves the ninety-nine and goes after the one sheep which is lost (Luke 15:4). Jesus had character: he was not a stereotype or religious clone. He enjoyed the company of those who did not fit in with the social and religious ideals of his day.

The scriptures place great value on the unique human individual. But this is very different from the way the individual is regarded in Western culture. Here the emphasis is less on value or uniqueness and more on the individual as isolated and independent. This view is reflected in the economic arrangement of our society in which the 'normal' individual is a separate 'unit of labour'. Deep in our intellectual tradition lies the statement of Descartes: 'I think therefore I am'. Nearer to the biblical view is the saying of African theologian, John Mbiti: 'I am because we are'.

A new-born child needs a community to become an adult. It is not merely that the child needs someone to provide food and clothing. In order to assume a personal and individual identity he or she needs to make their own the language, culture and social projects of a community. It is through and within this common possession that human individuality finds real expression. What is true generally – that individuals only attain a recognisable identity as part of a community – is also true of who we are spiritually.

In scripture we see individual lives lived as part of a corporate life. The Bible has its share of loners, people like Jeremiah, Elijah or John the Baptist, but even their aloneness is a way of participating in the common life. This way of thinking does not come naturally to us. It has sometimes been called 'corporate solidarity'. It is part of the fabric of biblical thought – so much so that whole communities are often personified as individuals. Jesus, like the prophets, addressed towns as well as individuals (Luke 10:13–15). He appointed the twelve to make clear the corporate identity of the church. He spoke of himself and the disciples as one vine (John 15).

Abraham and Jesus

Many people turn to John 3:16 to explain the gospel of Jesus Christ: the world is lost in sin and Jesus is God's way of salvation. The early Christians often started rather differently. For them, God's plan to save an idolatrous and rebellious world began with Abraham, a Mesopotamian city-dweller called to leave his country, family and way of life and to become the founder of a pilgrim people. As St Paul wrote, 'He is the father of us all' (Romans 4:16). God's plan of salvation is to create a people who will live in relationship with him, reflect his character and serve his purposes.

God's promise to Abraham was, 'In you shall all the nations be blessed' (Galatians 3:8, Genesis 12:3, RSV). After more than fifteen hundred years of preparation, this promise found its fulfilment in Jesus. Jesus is the second Adam. Standing with us in a fully human but sinless life, and in a lonely and sin-bearing death, he has become in his resurrection 'the firstborn among many brothers' (Romans 8:29), creating in himself 'a single new humanity' (Ephesians 2:15, NEB). Jesus' coming does not mean the abandonment of God's plan to create a people, but its fulfilment.

The coming of the Holy Spirit on the day of Pentecost was the reversal of the chaos and division of Babel, as the Holy Spirit began to draw people of every language into the people of God. The kingdom of God began to be experienced in a new way. For the first disciples – as we read in Acts – this was a bewildering as well as a costly experience. Life in the Spirit-filled church was neither perfect nor comfortable. In particular they had great difficulty in recognising the Spirit's acts as part of God's plan. Two thousand years later this difficulty comes to many Christians in a different form. They find it hard to see themselves as part of the church or to recognise older or different ways of expressing faith and worship as being filled with the Spirit.

REDISCOVERING THE CHURCH

Our blindness to the reality of the church has many roots. Some are cultural. Technological society has taught us to despise things from the past. Secular philosophy and economic structures blind us to the reality of the corporate. Cynicism and ignorance mean that we know too little about the beautiful service and life of Christians in other times and places.

Other barriers arise from history. In Britain the church is older than the nation and she is often seen as 'an irrelevant old grandmother', out of touch with the times. Either she is required to provide nostalgic colour for special occasions or resented for reminding us of ideals we would rather forget. More seriously, she is often identified with the sins of the established social order, even though historically she has often provided the voice of protest. Bishops attained their high profile in Western society by being the guardians of the poor.

Deeper barriers are theological. We expect the church to be sinless and discount it because of its many sins, although it only consists of sinful Christians like ourselves. Equally damaging is the claim that is sometimes made by Christian groups or by the institutional church that this *particular* church is the goal of God's purposes rather than its hope-filled and fallible servants.

One way to rediscover the church is to abandon the abstract world of concepts and get to know her as she is: the individuals, communities, adventures, triumphs and sorrows, acts of service, prayers, songs and writings that are her true glory. An important step in the growth of any Christian is the time he or she first looks out from the primary Christian group in which his or her Christian identity has been formed and recognises the life and activity of the Holy Spirit in the *different* ways of other Christians, past and present.

But what is 'the church'? Two pictures are sometimes used by Christians as they think about this question.

Two cities

Christians often see the church as God's alternative society, so that it becomes simply a place of refuge from the world. But according to the Bible, God's concern is *for* the world.

In his great work, *The City of God*, St Augustine wrote of the history of the world as the interwoven history of two cities or communities, which will exist alongside each other until the end of time. He takes as his starting point the biblical cities of Babylon and Jerusalem which scripture treats as symbolic of two ways of life and two human projects. The splendour of the heavenly city will not be revealed until Christ comes in glory. Its present life often passes unnoticed although it is full of beauty, holiness and love. This age is the age of the earthly city, which is built on the love of self and is symbolised by the pride of earthly Babylon (Genesis 11:1–9; Isaiah 13 and 14; Revelation 18). At the end of time the bankruptcy of the earthly city will be revealed, but in the meantime we are all inescapably citizens of this earthly city and it is the guardian of much human well-being.

Augustine does not suggest that we can or should withdraw from the earthly city. Christian discipleship means living out the tension of dual citizenship. Love of our neighbour means that we will work for the well-being of the earthly city. As Jeremiah wrote to the Jewish exiles in Babylon, 'Seek the peace and prosperity of the city to which [the Lord has] carried you into exile. Pray to the Lord for it, because if it prospers, you too will prosper' (Jeremiah 29:7).

The church is not so much an alternative society as a resistance movement. We are a company of people living in hostile territory: courageous but not foolish, cautious and shrewd, but willing to live dangerously and even to risk our lives. Wherever we can, we try to establish the values and love of our true allegiance. We are willing to take any opportunity to name the true King's name and to encourage others to do the same. We know that we shall often have set-backs but that one day the reign of love will come.

> Two cities have been formed by two loves; the earthly by the love of self, even to the contempt of God; the heavenly by the love of God, even to the contempt of self. The former glories in itself, the latter in the

> Lord . . . In the one, the princes and the nations it
> subdues are ruled by the love of ruling; in the other,
> the princes and the subjects serve one another in love.
>
> *St Augustine*

City or family?

Many Christians today find the picture of the family of God
the one which makes the church most real to them. The
human family is for many the place of refuge and belonging.
Here, at least, people are valued for what they are. Here, at
least, human contributions are simply given and received
rather than exchanged for money.

Because of the power of the picture of the church as
family, it is important to examine it carefully. The Greek
word in the New Testament which is often translated as
the word 'family' in English in fact means 'household'. The
household in those times was seen as a unit of society and
not a refuge from it. It included relatives, friends, other dependants and servants as well as parents and children. It formed
a microcosm of the city, not an alternative to it. In the tribal
society of Abraham, family and city were one. As society
developed, city and household became complementary modes
of common life – not alternatives.

Very different forces have shaped the modern ideal of the
family. Industrial society has tended to draw all human life
into its net so that human relationships and service have come
to be evaluated and exchanged in terms of money. Christians
and other social reformers have responded by elevating the
small unit of parents and children as the place of humanity
and belonging. We should not assume too easily that this
strategy has been successful. The modern image of the family
is partly the creation of commercial advertising and much of
family life is shaped to serve the demands of the commercial
market. For example, birth control has often been used not
to plan birth but to preserve the comfortable life-style of the
four members of the 'ideal' nuclear family.

Not only can the symbol of family be seen as the place
of self-love set apart from the wider human community, it

has other problems as well. Many people, perhaps most people, are not in 'standard' families. For young adults, the elderly, widows, gay people and single people, the symbol of the family can be one that oppresses and excludes. It serves to limit expectations and to restrict relationships – in particular friendships – which older societies valued and regarded as normal. Even for those in the modern 'family', the reality can be very far from its goal of humanity and belonging: life can be narrow and full of pain.

The symbol of family today is two-edged and must be used with care. It affirms values we should not lose; it can also blind us to the diversity of human life. Most seriously, it can become a refuge from the dual citizenship to which God calls the Christian.

1 Timothy 2 gives a picture of the early church at prayer. Some of the chapter reads very oddly in the light of much contemporary experience. The topics of prayer illustrate naturally the concern of these Christians for the earthly and the heavenly cities. Equally revealing are the seating arrangements. In the early church – as in many parts of the developing world today – families did not sit together. Men and women sat separately. This shows that, in the assembly of the church, people belong primarily to the community rather than to their biological families. (Even the controversial references to women are not quite what they seem and probably reflect the tensions that arose as Christian women found new dignity and freedom in the life of the church.)

CHRISTIAN WORSHIP

To belong to Christ is to belong to our fellow Christians. To belong to Christ is to be called to a dual citizenship. In the world we are to serve an unseen King. It is in gathering for worship that we see most truly who we are, 'a royal priesthood, a holy nation, a people belonging to God, that you may declare the praises of him who called you out of darkness into his wonderful light' (1 Peter 2:9). Our belonging together as 'a people' is a visible witness to the world. Christian private prayer is an extension of our public and corporate life. On our own, but part of the body of Christ, we open our lives to the Spirit of Christ and the hope of his kingdom.

Paul wrote, 'Your life is now hidden with Christ in God' (Colossians 3:3). Ultimately our Christian identity is a secret that waits for the revealing of Christ. However, it is displayed most clearly when Christ summons the church for worship. For this reason Christian private prayer must not be seen as unrelated to or more important than the public worship of the church. Individual prayer looks, of course, towards life in the world; even in this it is shaped by the call of God that we share with the rest of the church. The way that private prayer grows out of public worship can be seen very clearly in the part that Christian hymns and songs play in the private prayer of many Christians.

Martin Luther instructed Christians to recite each morning the Lord's Prayer and the Apostles' Creed, to say a prayer 'and then should'st thou go with joy to thy work, after a hymn or the Ten Commandments or whatever thy devotion may suggest'. Public worship feeds private prayer. Luther's reference to the Apostles' Creed provides an interesting example of this process. The Creed comes from the baptismal rite of the ancient Western Church. Before a person was baptised they learnt it by heart and then recited it before the gathered church to express the faith that brought them to baptism. From this it became for many centuries an integral part of the daily prayer of Christians.

The pattern of prayer
There is a tremendous variety to Christian worship, which takes its colour from the cultures, musical styles and social patterns of particular Christian groups. Within this variety there are fixed patterns which can be discerned.

There are four elements which impart a God-given, grace-centred shape to Christian worship. Christians gather on Sundays to celebrate the death and resurrection of Christ (Luke 24:1, Acts 20:7, 1 Corinthians 16:2). (This is church- and worship-based and must be distinguished from the family- and home-based institution of the Old Testament Sabbath.) The second element is baptism, which proclaims the gospel of Christ to both church and individual as a person is admitted to the life of the church. Third, the Lord's Supper, or

Eucharist, calls Christians into relationship with the death of Christ, with the living Christ and with each other. The fourth God-given element is the public reading of scripture (1 Timothy 4:13), which summons the church to listen to Christ and enriches and clarifies its grasp of the gospel.

If these four elements provide the skeleton of Christian worship, it is then fleshed out and clothed from the creative common life of the church. Many things determine the form that this takes. Some are theological: praise, remembering and petition are constant themes of biblical prayer. Some reflect our created human nature: words and music reflect human creativity; posture and movement help us express ourselves. Some are specific to particular cultures. Some determining factors are technological! The invention of cheap printing, for example, made possible congregational prayer and song books. This has strongly influenced Christian worship in the last two hundred years and has served both to enrich and to fix worship; it costs money to change a hymn book.

The pattern of worship can be compared to language. Both belong to the community, not to the individual, but thereby provide the individual with the means of self-expression and communication. Or again, forms of worship can be seen as a type of corporate art, rather like dance or community music in some cultures. The range of this corporate pattern is very wide; from simple prayers and songs, through larger and seasonal celebrations to solemn ceremonies. Sometimes groups of Christians become alienated from part of their common pattern. Often they find it hard to 'get inside' less familiar parts of the common pattern when it is needed; examples would be funerals or civic services. Often parts of the common pattern are seized on and used as rallying points by Christian groups in conflict.

Christian daily prayer is shaped by similar influences. Before the invention of personal watches, which helped to privatise time, Christians tended to pray at common times dictated by the routine of a household or the sound of the city crier or church bell. Prayer in the morning and at night reflects our human awareness of vulnerability at these

33

moments of natural transition. The invention of electric light has shifted this sense to later in the evening. (Winter darkness still lends a distinctive atmosphere to northern Christmases). Economic structures and work patterns have also played a part in privatising daily prayer.

Many Christians use short forms of daily prayer such as the Taizé office, Morning and Evening Prayer from the Anglican *Alternative Service Book,* the Roman Catholic Divine Office or *Celebrating Common Prayer.* These tend to draw on traditions of prayer from before the modern privatisation of daily prayer. A similar insight underlies some schemes that encourage daily Bible reading, such as those produced by Scripture Union or the Bible Reading Fellowship, which foster a sense of fellowship among those who use the material.

As we recognise the variety, the richness and the breadth of public worship which is our Christian heritage, we will have an environment in which our private prayer life can be enriched and grow. In our most private prayer, we are one with the church.

> No man is an *Island,* entire of it self; every man is a part of the *Continent,* a part of the *main* . . .
> *John Donne,* 1572–1631 (from *Meditation XVII*)

TAKE SEVEN DAYS . . .

Day 1 With the church

• Read 1 Corinthians 1:2–3. Notice how St Paul begins his letter with a reminder of the geographical and universal dimensions of the church and with the call and promise of the gospel.

Try to picture the Christian communities of your town or city and relate them to this passage. Then try to picture Christian congregations in other parts of the world. Let God help you to pray for some of these Christians.

• Read Hebrews 12:22–24. These words were written to some discouraged Jewish Christians who were feeling that their new life in Christ offered them less than their previous home in Judaism. It seemed to them less impressive (Hebrews 12:18–21) and less permanent or secure (Hebrews 12:25–29). Allow the images of verses 22–24 to grip you.

> Almighty God,
> you have knit together your elect
> into one communion and fellowship
>   in the mystical body of your Son.
> Give us grace so to follow your blessed saints
> in all virtuous and godly living,
> that we may come to those unspeakable joys
> which you have prepared for those who truly
>   love you;
> through Jesus Christ our Lord.
>
> *Collect for All Saints' Day*

Day 2 Baptism

• The twentieth century has seen various parts of the church struggling to rediscover the reality of baptism. Conversion disrupts life and it is therefore not surprising that the rediscovery of baptism is not a tidy process. Baptism means change for both the individual and the church. The body has to adjust to the arrival of a new member.

The water of baptism is a picture of the call and promise of God. Allow some of the following images to take hold of you. Notice how often there is a corporate dimension to the picture.

> Passing through judgement to eternal life (Luke 3:7;
>   1 Corinthians 10:1–2; 1 Peter 3:18–21)
> Cleansing and forgiveness (1 Corinthians 6:11)
> Renewal in the Spirit (Titus 3:5–7; Acts 2:33,38–39)
> New birth into the body of Christ (John 3:5; 1 Corinthians
>   12:12–13)
> Moving from death to life (Jonah 2:3–6, Romans 6:3–4)
> The unity of the church (Ephesians 4:4–5)

• Think first of those who sponsored you at your baptism and who have supported your life in the church. If baptism in your church tradition does not involve sponsors, think of those who have been your spiritual 'parents'. Ask what God is saying to you through the baptism that other Christians have received.

• Reflect on the following statement on baptism (from *Baptism, Eucharist and Ministry*) which was agreed in 1982 by all the major Christian traditions in Lima, Peru:

> Baptism is the sign of new life through Jesus Christ. It unites the one baptised with Christ and his people. The New Testament scriptures and the liturgy of the Church unfold the meaning of baptism in various images which express the riches of Christ and the gifts of his salvation . . . Baptism is both God's gift and our human response to that gift. It looks towards a growth into the measure of the stature of the fulness of Christ (Ephesians 4:13).

Day 3 Your kingdom come

• Imagine the meeting for worship you normally attend on a Sunday. Try to picture who is there and who feels most at home or left out. What people or topics will be prayed for?

• Read 1 Timothy 2:1–10. What topics did these Christians pray for? How did they see their place and calling in God's purposes? Allow the passage to guide you in prayer.

• Is there anything you can do to deepen or direct the prayer life of your church? Do you know what projects, Christian workers or organisations your church supports? Do you know much about them? Should they be part of your regular private prayer?

> Christ look upon us in this city
> And keep our sympathy and pity
> Fresh, and our faces heavenward
> Lest we grow hard.
>
> *Thomas Ashe*

Day 4 Sing us one of the songs of Zion

• Read Psalm 137:1–4.

• Find one or two hymns or songs that are important to a different generation or group of Christians than your own.

> Read or sing through them.
> If possible get someone for whom they are important to talk to you about them.
> Read through the hymns/songs quietly imagining the people and situations they represent.

Day 5 Until he comes

• Read 1 Corinthians 11:23–26. The scene is familiar. Jesus is accepting his lonely call to the cross. He gathers his apostles and bequeaths them this sign. He gives new significance to the shared bread which begins a Jewish meal and the shared cup which ends it. These actions which Jesus has given the church, and which Christians have enacted and interpreted in many different ways, have a very simple shape: saying grace and partaking, thanksgiving and communion.

Jesus' words – 'Do this in remembrance of me' – were addressed to the twelve apostles, the church in miniature, and not simply to individual Christians. Only corporate obedience is possible. To receive and obey Jesus' command the church has to be together.

1 Corinthians 11:17–22, 33–34 shows something of what this meant in one city. The Christians in Corinth may have met in different homes and groupings (1 Corinthians 1:11–12, 16:15,19) as well as together (Romans 16:23). The Eucharist brought them together in a way that made them face the differences, such as wealth and class, that divided them.

• Look at the order of service and prayers that your part of the church uses to celebrate the Lord's Supper.

> Can you see the shape of thanksgiving and communion?
> How are these two essential elements enacted in your church?

What do they mean for you and your fellow worshippers?

> For whenever you eat this bread and drink this cup,
> you proclaim the Lord's death until he comes.
>
> *1 Corinthians 11:26*

> Is not the cup of thanksgiving for which we give thanks
> a participation in the blood of Christ? And is not the
> bread that we break a participation in the body of
> Christ? Because there is one loaf, we, who are many,
> are one body, for we all partake of the one loaf.
>
> *1 Corinthians 10:16–17*

> Love each other as I have loved you.   *John 15:12*

Day 6 Honour and remember

• Read Philippians 2:25–30, Acts 9:36–41 and Hebrews
13:7. Remembering is a very important aspect of biblical
faith and remembering God's work through individuals is
part of this.

> Who do Epaphroditus or Dorcas remind you of?
> Who were the Christians who brought you the word
>   of God or who have given you an example of faith?
> What do you know about the history of your church and
>   of other churches in your town or city?
> Who first brought the message of Christ to your town
>   and country? Remember and give thanks for those
>   whom God brings to mind.

• Find out who the heroes are of Christians you know. Are
there Christians of the past you ought to be learning about?
There are two traps it is easy to fall into. One is to use
past figures as rallying points without understanding the real
meaning of their lives (Matthew 23:29–30). Another is not
noticing how wonderfully varied, eccentric and imperfect
God's servants are.

Day 7 The new Jerusalem

• Read Revelation 21:1–14 and 21:22–22:5. What might

this vision mean to different people? For example:

St John in exile on an island in the Aegean (Revelation
   1:9)
a poor widow in the slums of Brazil
a Christian artist or poet or gardener
a politician struggling to improve society
a ten year-old child
a Christian in prison for their faith in Turkey or Nepal
someone planning to retire after a successful career
a Christian pastor
a Christian dying of hunger in an African nation where
   there is famine
a young worker
a young family who find managing on social security
   difficult
members of a Christian co-operative in a Mexican slum

Bring the different feelings and people that this has evoked
to God.

> Almighty God, you have entrusted this earth to the
> children of men, and through your Son Jesus Christ
> have called us to a heavenly citizenship; grant us such
> shame and repentance for the disorder, injustice and
> cruelty which are among us, that, fleeing to you for
> pardon and grace, we may henceforth set ourselves to
> establish that city which has justice for its foundation
> and love for its law, of which you are the architect and
> builder; through the same Jesus Christ, your Son, our
> Lord. Amen.

> Merciful God,
> you have prepared for those who love you
> such good things as pass man's understanding.
> Pour into our hearts such love towards you
> that we, loving you above all things,
> may obtain your promises,
> which exceed all that we can desire;
> through Jesus Christ our Lord. Amen.
> *Collect for the last Sunday after Pentecost*

3

THE DAILY MIRROR

Colin Matthews

'Sometimes I'm too scared to open my Bible. I'm afraid it may tell me something about myself I'd rather not know, or ask me to do something I can't cope with.'

Going to the Bible to find the truth may sound like a comfortable thing to do but, as the sophisticated student who said this revealed, a willingness to face the truth may take considerable courage and honesty. Yet if spiritual development is to lead to genuine growth in maturity it must be based on scriptural truth. Without this voice from outside ourselves, explorations of spirituality may become merely exercises in escapism, self-indulgence or sentimentality.

THE TRUTH MAKES US CHOOSE

Jesus once said to some questioners who tried to catch him out, 'You are in error because you do not know the Scriptures or the power of God' (Matthew 22:29). So what sort of truth does the Bible give us?

First, it tells a true story: the story of God's love for his people. It tells this story through the history of particular people, and is therefore full of characters, times and places. In the course of this story it describes the lives of the people who are caught up in it. Above all, the Bible reveals to us the character of the one true God who is the Father of the Lord Jesus Christ.

Second, the Bible presents us with values to choose

between. Some choices are set out clearly and unambiguously (do this, don't do that, God is like this, he is not like that). Others are more subtly expressed (here are people who pleased God, follow their example; here are values and principles that you must live by, but you must work out what particular action is required in your situation).

The truth the Bible presents to us is not therefore just a collection of statements or a true record of events. It is a statement about reality, a description of the way things are. Ultimately, it is a revelation of the truth about God. We can choose to face reality or to run from it. Our choice will shape our lives.

> Just as everything outside us originates in the word of God, so does everything inside us. We can't get behind the word of God. There is no human insight, no human desire, no human cry anterior to this word of God. There is no great abstraction, no great truth behind or previous to this word. Everywhere we look, everywhere we probe, everywhere we listen we come upon *word* – and it is God's word, not ours.
>
> *Eugene Peterson*

A senior executive in a multinational company was an expert in finance. He knew how money worked. Although a Christian for a number of years, he kept his money firmly in his own hands. The amount of money he gave away was controlled and limited.

Then he was challenged to take seriously what the Bible said about money: to face the reality of how God sees money. He began to ask God's help to know how to earn it, how to spend it – and how to give it away. As a result he resigned from a directorship on a matter of principle and he also took seriously what the Bible said about making giving to God's work a priority. He says that it was only then that he began to develop as a person and as a Christian.

As we choose, God responds. Sometimes the choice seems hard and costly and may indeed prove to be so in its outworking. But always God surprises us by his grace.

A man in his twenties became a Christian and knew that

the consequence of that decision was that Jesus should be Lord of his sexuality. This meant that the sexual relationship with his girlfriend must stop, even though they cared very much for each other. He dreaded sharing his decision with his girlfriend but knew it had to be done. As he began to share, however, his girlfriend began crying. She too was a Christian, but one who had run away from God. She had been struggling with great feelings of guilt for a number of years. Her boyfriend's honesty and courage brought her back to the Lord. They were then able to seek God's future for their relationship.

Perhaps their story sounds too romantic and sentimental. Not every story of obedience leads to an immediate happy ending. But obedience is the vital first step towards real life.

> In the understanding of Israel, repentance meant a change of social behaviour as evidence of a fresh commitment to God. And the prophets were very specific about it. It is evident in Jeremiah as it is in John the Baptist. Zaccheus understood it and acted accordingly, and the so-called rich young ruler also understood it.
> *Samuel Escobar*

Throughout this book there will be many references to feelings, images and impressions. All these need to be brought back to the scriptures to be tested. God's Spirit never contradicts himself. He will not lead us or guide us in ways which are at odds with the scriptures he inspired, however much we try to persuade ourselves to the contrary. To know the scriptures is to know the mind of Christ.

The truth that the Bible sets before us is not neutral. It challenges us to make choices and therefore has the power to change our lives. Our decisions have consequences; God himself responds to our choices. We can choose to let him move us on in his light or we can choose to stay in the shadows.

THE TRUTH FACES US WITH REALITY
The truth of God comes to us as a mirror (James 1:23) or a light (Psalm 119:105) or a hammer (Jeremiah 23:29) or

a sword (Hebrews 4:12). Sometimes its message will be as sweet as honey (Ezekiel 3:3), at other times it will burn us up with its intensity (Jeremiah 20:9). In these ways we see that the Bible first informs our understanding and then asks us to decide how to live on the basis of the truth we have seen. The Bible brings us face to face with God and so face to face with ourselves.

> Do not merely listen to the word, and so deceive your-
> selves. Do what it says. Anyone who listens to the
> word but does not do what it says is like a man who
> looks at his face in a mirror and, after looking at
> himself, goes away and immediately forgets what he
> looks like. But the man who looks intently into the
> perfect law that gives freedom, and continues to do
> this, not forgetting what he has heard, but doing it –
> he will be blessed in what he does.   *James 1:22–25*

For some people an encounter with the truth is exhilarating and liberating: 'Come, see a man who told me everything I ever did. Could this be the Christ?' (John 4:29). The truth of the good news of Jesus was welcomed by a woman who hitherto had sought self-discovery and personal fulfilment mainly through her sexuality. Jesus offered her the opportunity to come to maturity by choosing to live by the truth of God and to give herself in worship. For the rich young ruler the encounter with reality was more than he could bear: 'Go, sell everything you have and give to the poor, and you will have treasure in heaven. Then come, follow me' (Mark 10:21).

A JOURNEY INTO REALITY
Perhaps it all sounds too simple. Life rarely presents a series of black and white choices. More often there seems to be a series of choices in varying shades of grey. Several principles may help us.

• We must find out what the Bible *really* means – not what we wish it would say.

• We must trust God sufficiently to be willing to seek the truth with the whole of our lives. A Christian is a person whose life has been opened to the truth, opened to Jesus. To be a Christian means to start a journey based on truth. It may be hard, slow, painful and demanding. It will also be exhilarating, disturbing and full of joy.

• We must be willing to *act* on what we are shown, believing that it is only as we obey that we are led forward.

So how do we go on this journey into reality? The first thing to realise is that it is a journey and, like any journey, it's not instant, it takes time. And where do we start? The answer, as always, is at the cross – the cross where God made his shocking response to what you and I are really like. But there we are welcomed, held, secured. In Jesus we are accepted. There is now nothing in ourselves or in God to run from. He has seen it all, he knows it all, he has forgiven it all, he will transform it all. We are so secure in Christ, therefore, that there is nothing in ourselves and in our world that we cannot now face.

Often we experience life as uncomfortable, so we go to the Bible for comfort and reassurance. Life is difficult and we need to be sure that God is with us, that he lives and cares for us – that he is in control, and will see us safely through. And God, in his sovereign greatness and mercy, meets us at these points of need. Part of growing as a Christian, part of maturing as a person (the two are the same), is to come to Jesus with those parts of ourselves which we may be ashamed of because they seem 'weak'. All of us often need to hear the words of the risen Jesus, 'Peace be with you'.

However, precisely because we often experience life as hard and unpleasant, our need to find comfort can cause us to distort our use of the Bible in a number of ways.

First, we can be in danger of making our reading of the Bible into a constant search for a passage, phrase, verse or idea which will 'make us feel better'. We treat the Bible as a sort of divine 'chocolate box': a collection of sweets to suck for comfort and security. So we skim over pages and pages of text until we find something that meets our need. In the end this leads to a Christian life which is built on human need, 'my need', and not on truth. Our desire is to grow in comfort, not in wisdom.

A second pitfall is to go to the Bible to find quick and easy answers. We have a choice to make and we want the Bible to work for us like a super-computer. Key in the problem and the text with the answer will come up on the screen. Thank God that when we abuse the Bible in this way, he often does guide us simply and directly – because he is more concerned about our choices than we are.

Alternatively, we may see our Bibles as toasters, expecting a nicely cooked text to pop up to start the day, so that we do not have to do our part in praying, listening, understanding and testing.

USING THE BIBLE FOR GUIDANCE

Using the Bible rightly is a vital part of guidance, but what's the complete picture? Many Christians would say that in their experience the Holy Spirit guides them through ...

the Bible
Christian leaders
the gifts of the Spirit, eg wisdom, discernment
learning from past experiences
the advice of friends
circumstances
personal convictions
prayer

When we have decisions to make, it is important to use all of these approaches in order to hear what God is saying. However, the Bible is not just one way amongst several ways. It is the Bible which equips leaders to be effective in leadership (2 Timothy 3:16–17); which shows the way to use the gifts of the Spirit; which helps us to evaluate past experiences. We need friends who are themselves wise in the scriptures. The Bible helps us to set our priorities, and shapes our personal convictions as we take scripture to heart. And the Bible informs and directs our prayers and inspires us to pray.

How does the Bible do this? First, by laying down the ground rules; second, by helping us to see what God likes and dislikes, to see the things that matter to him. Above all, we read the Bible in order to get to know God better. In practice, therefore, when we need to make a major decision we should ask ourselves these questions:

What does the Bible say about my situation?
What do leaders I trust advise?
What can I learn from God's work in my life so far?
What do my friends think?
How can I see God at work in my present circumstances?
What are my own feelings?
How should I pray?

As we ask such questions and find their answers, we should expect the Spirit who inspired the scriptures to bring these things together. It won't always be easy. But given time, the hand print of God will be seen.

In response to these misuses, we will want to learn how to use the Bible correctly, so that we are given a reliable foundation not a false peace. If we are to grow as Christians, we have to face up to the 'real truth' about God as he is, ourselves as we are and will be, and our world as it is and as it is becoming.

It may be that the truth is the last thing we want to find. This is why some Christians and Christian groups lose themselves in fantasy. They go to church not to face reality but to escape from it. 'The only reason a Christian is ill is because they don't have enough faith.' 'God wants every Christian in business to succeed and be wealthy.' 'The Lord has chosen our country and our government to prosper in his world.' And it is all attractive, powerful, popular fantasy.

This book is designed to help develop attitudes, habits and disciplines which will help Christians to see clearly; to understand, (not just with their minds but with their imaginations, emotions, wills and actions) what is right, what is true, what is just; to build on the Rock, not to play on the sand. There will be many obstacles to overcome. Honest people are not comfortable people. We prefer tact to honesty! Jesus was not comfortable, although he was comforting – and honest. Because he was honest, his main enemy was hypocrisy; and hypocrisy, particularly in ourselves, will be our enemy too. Jesus opposed hypocrisy precisely because it was a denial of the truth, of reality. It was a denial motivated by greed, fear, pride or a hunger for power; or to preserve a selfish vested interest. Can such hypocrisy ever be found in ourselves?

Of course, God in his mercy doesn't show us all the truth about ourselves at once. If he did, it would kill us. He knows how much of the truth we can bear. As we respond to what we are shown, so we are led forward. We shall not see him as he is until we are made as we should be. So far we have been concerned with questions about ourselves; *our* concerns, *our* interests, *our* needs. But here, as always, the initiative for the truth lies with God himself.

SOME PRACTICAL GUIDELINES
If we want to use the Bible to see reality we shall have to learn how to look at it clearly. So what's needed?

Make time ... and act!
We need to listen to God each day and we need resolve to act on what we hear. We need to make time for God and his word each day so that there is a firm objective base at the centre of our lives. This time alone with God each day is just part of the story. As part of our 'rule of life' we may need to plan other types of 'time for God' (maybe weekly, monthly or yearly; maybe on our own or with others; maybe at home, at church or on retreat).

Use the Bible

We need to learn how to use the Bible effectively. This sounds like hard work, and perhaps it is! However, if we're to avoid making the Bible say only what we want to hear, we need to let it speak to us first on its own terms. This means that our readings should be based on a wide selection of passages, not just on the 'family favourites'. Although sometimes we may follow a theme or one character's story, our main emphasis should be on reading the Bible books in their original shape. We need to be concerned to find out what the passage *says* before going on to ask what it *requires*.

This last point is particularly important. We all know the dangers of 'taking a verse out of context' – but that doesn't mean we don't still do it! And we have all heard preachers who use the Bible like a springboard – one fleeting touch before leaping off on their own! Letting the Bible speak in its own terms means trying to answer honestly three questions:

• What is the natural meaning? (What do the English words mean, without any fancy interpretation?)

• What is the original meaning? (What would those to whom the words were first addressed have understood them to mean?)

• What is the general meaning? (This means comparing the meaning of one part of the Bible with that of another.)

Obviously this can take a little time! One of the reasons for using Bible reading notes, therefore, is that a lot of this background work is done for you.

All this may sound a little cold and clinical. Elsewhere in this book you will find ideas about how to use the Bible for meditation, prayer and worship, exciting ideas to stretch and develop our gifts of imagination and creativity. However, if through these methods we 'get out' of the Bible things that were never 'in there' in the first place, then we are in danger of fantasy.

God speaks

We need to discover how God speaks to us through the Bible.

As we have seen already, what God says today through the Bible must be linked to his original intention for the scriptures; but we need to go further.

How does God guide us through the scriptures? Sometimes a text will 'come up and hit us', but generally he guides us in two ways. First, he gives us clear principles and guidelines. We do not need to keep asking, 'Is it wrong to steal?' 'Is it good to pray for my family?' God has answered these questions once and for all. Second, he guides us by showing us more and more of his character and personality. As we get to know him through the work of the Holy Spirit, we get a sense of what he likes and dislikes. This is another reason for reading widely in the Bible: we will discover all the aspects of God's character.

However, as James reminds us in chapter 1 of his letter, we understand the truth of the Bible not just by thinking about it but by living it and reflecting on our experience of doing so. We will never learn how to drive a car, fall in love or bring up children simply by reading books. We learn from experience – and sometimes it's not always too comfortable!

> As we address scripture, scripture addresses us. We find that our culturally conditioned presuppositions are being challenged and our questions corrected. In fact, we are compelled to reformulate our previous questions and to ask fresh ones. So the living interaction proceeds.
>
> *The Willowbank Report* (Scripture Union)

This pattern of learning and growth applies to all levels: to great truths and little ones. However, throughout the Bible there seems to be one area in which action and reflection are particularly important, and that is our commitment to help the poor and those who suffer injustice. Often, and rightly, we think of helping others because of their needs; but unless we get used to looking at life 'from the underside' (seeing it from the perspective of those who are 'losers' in this world) we shall not see the Bible the right way up; we shall not see the truth. Our involvement alongside those who are least in the world's eyes will change our understanding.

Our commitment to them will help us to see clearly. The 'losers' need the 'winners' to find hope; the 'winners' need the 'losers' to see truth.

> We will have to acknowledge that subjects like justice, poverty, and oppression are not accidental departures, here and there, from the great lines of biblical teaching. To our surprise they may be inseparable from the great themes of revelation, relationship with God, repentance and the essence of Christian life ... I cannot avoid feeling that when I read some evangelical writers who defend capitalism, discarding serious criticism, I see them falling into the trap that Brian Griffiths has described: 'The temptation facing each one of us is to interpret Jesus's teaching to fit our preconceived ideas on these matters or else simply to justify our present lifestyle and interests.'
> *Samuel Escobar*

Look back!

We need to look back on the journey to learn from the past. There are various ways of doing this. Many people find it helpful to plan into their lives a day (or even a week) at regular intervals to make time to 'stock-take'. Many find it helpful to keep some form of journal or notebook on a daily, weekly or occasional basis. Somehow the act of writing things down gives a reality and objective focus to our use of the Bible. You may like to consider using a journal like this for a week or a month or a year simply as an exercise to focus your own use of the Bible. Every week or month it is important to work back over the previous entries to reflect on the journey you have taken and to sense God's new adventures for your life. Chapter thirteen has more on journalling.

Be honest!

- We need to develop an attitude of honesty.

- We need to be honest about our doubts and difficulties.

- We should never be afraid to ask questions, however hard,

of the Bible. What matters is the way in which we ask them. If we are hard, scornful, arrogant and demanding, then we won't find answers. If we are honest, seeking, patient and humble, then God will lead us forward.

• We need to be honest about our desires.

• We need to be honest about our failures.

• We need to be honest in our approach to the text, not imposing our views but testing them.

• We need to be honest with others.

This chapter may have given the impression that reading the Bible to get at the truth is a personal and private journey, but in this, as in other aspects of following Christ, we need the help of our sisters and brothers in Christ. This may require a certain costly willingness on our part, a willingness to be accountable, to share our discoveries with our friends and allow them the space and time to be honest in their response.

It's better together

> Let the peace of Christ rule in your hearts, since as members of one body you were called to peace. And be thankful. Let the word of Christ dwell in you richly as you teach and admonish one another with all wisdom, and as you sing psalms, hymns and spiritual songs with gratitude in your hearts to God. And whatever you do, whether in word or deed, do it all in the name of the Lord Jesus, giving thanks to God the Father through him. *Colossians 3:15–17*

We sometimes read these verses as though God's guidance is only a matter of doing 'what feels good'. These verses, read in their context, clearly show that the 'peace of God' is not just feelings of peace in ourselves but harmony and co-operation in the fellowship. So we test the truth of our guidance and of our choices on what is good for us – individually and corporately – together with all God's people.

We also need to study the Bible together, particularly where Christians are divided on an issue. Then it is essential that we seek the truth together, sharing our views of the scriptures in trust, humility and acceptance, and in a spirit of honest enquiry. This may not lead to instant unanimity or even agreement. However, a willingness to change where we can be shown to be wrong is the only way to move forward into the truth together. As a way of checking our own prejudices and blind spots, it's also very valuable to look for opportunities to read and study the Bible together with Christians from other countries or backgrounds.

Listen to God

This chapter is about reading the Bible, but reading the Bible is never an end in itself. We read the Bible to find the truth – the truth about God. This can be described as 'listening to God'.

Listening to God can start when we make space in our lives for him to speak, when we find a place to be still so that we can see and understand, a place of sense when our lives seem to make no sense. To listen to God is simply to give him space and time and stillness. We do not need to *make* him speak. He has already promised to do so. All we need to do is to come to the place in our lives where we are willing to listen. Listening to God means more than reading the text. It means facing not just the text but the inspirer of that text – God. So we come with worship and thanksgiving. We come determined to give our best attention to God and open to all he has to say, however hard or unexpected that may be.

Listening to God as we read the Bible means that we come to him expecting to hear something new, living and fresh – a word that has never existed before it was spoken to us. Of course, this will not be a new word of doctrine or commandment – the Holy Spirit does not contradict himself – but it will be a new word of life and truth, which goes beyond the page to our hearts and minds.

To make ourselves vulnerable to the word of God in this way will sometimes be a struggle. Reading the text is merely a task to do. Listening requires a personal encounter with the Author. We read a newspaper. We listen to a letter from a friend for whom we care deeply. When we read a newspaper, we hear in our minds our own voice. When we read a letter, we hear the voice of our friend.

And what truth will we hear? Who knows? That is for the sovereign God to decide. That is the adventure. That is the excitement.

TAKE SEVEN DAYS . . .

Day 1 Looking in the mirror

• Read James 1:22–25. As you look into the mirror of God's word, let it lead you into . . .

> confession
> thanksgiving
> prayer for today
> action

• James 1:25 talks about 'the man . . . who continues to do this'. Many people find it helpful to plan into their diary regular specific times for Bible reading, prayer and reflection. Sometimes this is known as the 'rule of life'. Take time to see how you could give greater priority to opening your life to God's truth. (You will find more help to do this in *A Rule of Life?* by Harold Miller, published by Grove Books, 1984.)

Day 2 The cutting edge

• Read Hebrews 4:12–13. How honest are you in really wanting to understand and follow God's way for your life? Spend some time working through the following five questions:

1   Looking back over the past twelve months, can you name specific attitudes or actions which you have changed because of what you have seen in the Bible?

2   When you read the Bible, are you willing for God to

make you uncomfortable or are you mainly looking for comfort?

3   Looking back over the past twelve months, have you opened your life to a wide variety of scripture passages or restricted your contact mainly to passages which were already familiar to you?

4   Have you been willing to test out your understanding of the Bible with other people, even if you know they may not share your understanding of what it means?

5   If it could be shown to you that an action or an attitude of yours was clearly inconsistent with the Bible, would you be willing to change? What evidence do you have in your life that this is indeed the case?

Spend some time reflecting on your answers and turn your thoughts into prayer.

Day 3 Hammer and fire

• Meditate on the words of Jeremiah 23:29.

• 'Sometimes I'm too scared to open my Bible.' Write a letter in response to the student who made this statement. Try to make as many references as you can to the Bible itself and also to your own experience.

• Are there any words from the Bible which are like fire or a hammer for you at the moment? How will you respond?

Day 4 Sweet as honey

• Meditate on the words of Ezekiel 3:3 and Romans 15:4.

• Do you remember any times of difficulty or crisis that you have experienced? What Bible verses were especially helpful to you at those times? Write those verses down and describe how and why they brought you encouragement.

Are there any particular Bible verses that you believe God is using to comfort and encourage you at the present time? Write these down too.

- Try keeping a daily record of your thoughts and responses as you read God's word over the next three or four days. There is more about keeping a spiritual journal in chapter thirteen.

Day 5 Light of life

- Meditate on the following passage:

> For Christians the beginning of the day should not be burdened and oppressed with besetting concerns for the day's work. At the threshold of the new day stands the Lord who made it. All the darkness and distraction of the dreams of night retreat before the clear light of Jesus Christ and his wakening Word. All unrest, all impurity, all care and anxiety flee before him. Therefore, at the beginning of the day let all distraction and empty talk be silenced and let the first thought and the first word belong to him to whom our whole life belongs. 'Awake thou that sleepest, and arise from the dead, and Christ shall give thee light' (Ephesians 5:14).   *Dietrich Bonhoeffer*

- Resolve to set aside time each day to open your life to the light of God's word. If you don't already use some form of Bible study notes or guide, consider doing so. (For a free sample booklet introducing three Scripture Union guides, send a stamped, addressed envelope to: Samplers for Bible reading notes, The Marketing Department, Scripture Union, 130 City Road, London EC1V 2NJ.)

Day 6 Images of the word

- Consider the following images of God's word:

    a mirror (James 1:23)
    a sword (Hebrews 4:12)
    a hammer (Jeremiah 23:29)
    a fire (Jeremiah 20:9)
    honey (Ezekiel 3:3)
    light (Psalm 119:105)

How could each of them help you to use the Bible more effectively?

• Respond to each image of God's word by writing a poem, a prayer or a song, or by drawing a picture.

Day 7 'Your word is truth'

• Use the three questions below (see also page 00) to study one or more of the following passages: Psalm 42; Psalm 63; Isaiah 6:1–10; Jeremiah 13:1–11; Matthew 4:1–11; Luke 10:38–42; John 14:15–27; John 15:1–17.

> What is the natural meaning? (What do the English words mean, without any fancy interpretation?)
>
> What is the original meaning? (What would those to whom the words were first addressed have understood them to mean?)
>
> What is the general meaning? (This means comparing the meaning of one part of the Bible with that of another.)

• Let this prayer of Jesus for his disciples inspire your own prayer.

> Sanctify them by the truth; your word is truth.
>
> *John 17:17*

4

KEEPING COMPANY WITH GOD

Graham Pigott

Praying is being in relationship with God, living with God, being yourself with God, and letting God be himself with you. Dom Chapman is often quoted as saying, 'Pray as you can, not as you can't.'

Beginning is often the most difficult part of praying. Discovering our lack of desire, or weakness in self-discipline, can easily lead to a sense of guilt, a feeling that we have failed or don't know how to pray 'properly'. That is why the larger and looser definitions of praying which I began with are so important. If our conscious, or perhaps unconscious, image of praying is too closely linked to a particular style or technique we have learnt, this may stop us recognising other ways of praying, of being in relationship with God and open to receive from God. So let's begin at the beginning.

PRAYER – GOD'S ACTIVITY IN US

> Prayer is not another part for us to act, another skill for us to master . . . it is a relationship, a relationship with God.   *Simon Tugwell*
>
> We do not control good prayer by our preparations, but only dispose ourselves for it. God does the rest.
>   *Margaret Hebblethwaite*

When we seek to pray, we are giving our attention, however weak, to God who is always there to give himself to each of us. Before ever we pray, the risen Lord Jesus Christ is forever praying for us (Hebrews 7:25, Romans 8:34). Likewise in all our struggling and longing, the Spirit is ever at work in us (Romans 8:26–27). All Christian prayer is the gift of the Spirit, through Christ to the Father. Prayer, then, is more about his activity in us than our efforts for him! We are on the receiving end of his love. In prayer we begin to recognise and receive this and consciously enter into the relationship he is forever offering us and secretly sustains in us.

Beginning this way we can see our contribution more clearly in context. Our approaches and preferences can vary enormously and the other chapters in this book will reveal this. It is appropriate to use whatever we find helpful to become aware of God's presence, to express our desires and devotion, and to respond to his initiatives. When we seek to pray, we are opening ourselves to the Father who loves us and listens to us; to the Son who came into this world to serve us and now intercedes for us; and to the Spirit who prays within us, drawing us towards God our Father and Jesus our Lord. It is Almighty God – in all his richness as Father, Son and Holy Spirit – who is helping us to give ourselves back to himself through prayer.

PRAYER – OUR DESIRING

Having begun by outlining God's activity and initiative we can begin to recognise the place of our own desiring. We can also begin to appreciate why prayer in various forms is found in all religions and reflects a very human need to love, ask and seek beyond ourselves. God has created in us a restlessness, a desiring, a longing, a searching, which finds satisfaction and fulfilment only in God himself. However, in our spiritual exploring there can be many distractions and deviations. We can be tempted by alternatives to be satisfied with less than God himself, lured into false securities and preoccupations. We all have disordered desires, often manipulated by the media and advertising images, as well as a jumbled inheritance of experiences through our home, education, upbringing and work experience. These often include impressions of God that are less than Christian.

PRAYER – A PERSONAL PILGRIMAGE

In prayer we engage in the life-long pilgrimage of sifting and searching, asking and seeking, and finding, to our encouragement and delight, that God is already working within us, wanting our consent for his Spirit to be wedded to our spirit and express his life in all our living. When we pray, we are letting this happen, giving our desiring and searching a more Christian shape, with the God and Father of our Lord Jesus Christ as our focus.

> Let Jesus be in your heart,
> Eternity in your spirit,
> The world under your feet,
> The will of God in your actions,
> And let the love of God shine forth from you.
>
> *St Catherine of Genoa*

Prayer, then, is a profoundly divine and human activity, which penetrates the whole of us – body, mind, emotions and spirit – all interacting and being drawn towards God, however vaguely perceived in our own understanding and experience. As we develop as Christians, our previous kinds of praying are given this new and known focus, and God our Father can work more profoundly in us by his Spirit, with our consent, making us in character and being more like his Son, Jesus our Lord (2 Corinthians 3:18). So take heart! The very fact that you are reading this book at this moment is a sign of your searching and desire, and evidence, too, of the movement of God's Spirit within you!

PRAYER IN PRACTICE

God is always with us but we are not always aware of being with him. We may have moments of awareness during a day when we ask for help or give thanks for something special. Our praying is to be this personal and, in part, unpredictable, happening in any place and at any time as we are suddenly open to God. We may hum a hymn tune, sing a chorus, remember a verse of scripture or make a special request. Prayer can take many forms as we express our growing hope and trust in God.

> Praying is not some tight exercise, with sore knees and a bad back, fingers pushed hard against each other, eyes screwed up, mind ticking vigorously through a prescribed course. Prayer is an exploration of all our faculties as channels towards God, and we will not explore very far unless we wander and experiment and stretch ourselves.
>
> *Margaret Hebblethwaite*

Jesus' example

Praying our way through life can be very informal. But it was because Jesus stopped to pray in special places that the disciples asked for help, wanting to know the secret of Jesus' spontaneity and depth of devotion (Luke 11:1–2). When we look at Jesus' pattern, we can see that he went to the local synagogues to pray with other Jews, the pilgrim people of God, and learnt from their common prayer tradition through sharing in the services. So Jesus knew the psalms, many sections of scripture and the great prayers of his Jewish heritage. He probably used a Jewish prayer shawl, raised his hands in the air at times when standing for prayer, prayed aloud as well as silently in his mind and spirit, sat, knelt and bowed down or lifted his eyes towards heaven. All that he learnt in this way he took into his private praying on the hills (Mark 6:46). Jesus spoke his prayers aloud in the Garden of Gethsemane (Luke 22:39–46) and knelt and sweated in great turmoil. He prayed with the whole of himself, in a variety of ways, giving himself back to God his Father, fulfilling the most important commandment: to love God with everything we are (Mark 12:29–30).

It is this stopping to pray with the whole of ourselves, as Jesus did, that deepens our devotion and helps us to draw on the rich well-springs of our Christian heritage. As we take time to pray, we will find it is God who is prompting us, making prayer possible by his Spirit assisting our spirit. So, when we pray we are never spiritually alone. Whether in physical solitude or not, whether in deep distress or not, we share in the risen life of Christ, his Church and his Spirit, and the whole of the heavenly host is silently and invisibly with us.

Stopping to start

Stopping whatever we are doing to start praying is essential to enable an awareness of being with God to develop. However, in the bustle of living, stopping can be the hardest thing to do. Eventually even our informal spontaneous praying can wither up with weariness and die.

The way forward lies in finding for ourselves what helps us to stop, be still and start praying. This will vary not only from person to person, but also at the various stages of life. What is helpful to a commuter may not suit a mother at home caring for young children, a lorry driver or a seventeen year-old student at school. We each have to find our own way, and the other chapters in this handbook will introduce some of the many possibilities that can be tried. However, it is important to settle for a basic pattern because good habits in prayer help us to be aware of, and more receptive to, the presence of God. Reviewing our chosen pattern every few months can help our preparations for prayer to evolve in harmony with what God's Spirit is prompting and shaping within us. The effects of these special times of prayer will soon spill over into all our living, releasing again a new spontaneity with God and awareness of him.

> Every morning put your mind into your heart and stand in the presence of God all day long.
>
> *An Eastern monk*

Staying in prayer

If stopping in order to start is the first major step to praying regularly, staying in prayer is the second most common and very human difficulty. Our thoughts tend to wander and we may find settling into a relaxed form of concentration or awareness seemingly impossible. We may be distracted by the activities and noises around us, as well as the flurry of fleeting thoughts or pressing anxieties within us. For this reason our preparation for and approaches to our special prayer times are important. They will help us with these very difficulties. Always remember, however, that prayer is God's gift to us and his activity in us. Our part is to make ourselves available to him in a relaxed and attentive way, learning to listen from the centre of ourselves and accept, sift and offer the varied responses which well up within us. The distractions we experience may be signs of a deeper healing that is happening and a clue to the significant struggles within us. As we offer ourselves and our concerns to God in prayer, our jumble and disorder will often surface in these ways as part of this process. So again take heart! God is in the recycling business, forming out of the disorder and chaos in each of us his new creation in the likeness of Christ.

SOME WAYS OF BEGINNING

Most of the ways into prayer which are briefly touched on here will be developed in more detail in other chapters. The purpose of suggesting these ways into prayer is to help you, first, to stop and make some specific preparation for prayer and, second, to stay in a prayerful openness to God's presence, listening and letting your awareness of and love for him grow. Sometimes you may experience barrenness or tiredness, or difficulty in settling and concentrating. Such struggles are common and an authentic part of learning to pray. Many of our difficulties with distractions can be used by God to heal and renew us. For this reason these particular approaches have proved to be helpful ways of seeking to be in God's presence.

Finding a place

Where can you hope to find a quiet place? Perhaps in a favourite chair or in the corner of a room? You may try inside or outside, at home, or in church, by a window or sitting in the car or even the corner of a railway carriage! By having a regular place you will begin to associate being there with praying. By contrast, when you are out of routine you can use the very place you are in as a starting point for prayer as the circumstance itself suggests. You may be sitting on the beach watching the sea, or waiting for the doctor, or strap-hanging in the underground! Learning to be inwardly attentive in one place will help you to be open to God in other places.

Choosing a time
This is a twofold decision, deciding both when and for how long you will pray. Finding what will suit your pattern of life may take a while, so experiment with different times, in the morning, at lunch time and in the evening. When can you hope to have ten to twenty minutes without interruptions? Be honest and compassionate with yourself. A few minutes is better than none. A short time, daily, helps to develop a good habit which can grow with practice as you discover the ways into prayer which you prefer.

Discovering a posture
Avoid being uncomfortable! Bent forward with a cramped stomach and your head in your hands is not at all helpful, unless you are very distressed, because such a position prevents relaxed breathing. With the decline of the tradition of kneeling in church the 'bowed head crouch' has become an unfortunate norm which others unwittingly copy. For relaxed concentration sitting with a straight back, feet flat on the floor, using a comfortable upright chair, is a good position and posture. Keep your hands loosely open, palms upward resting in your lap. But also try lying down, standing and kneeling, especially with a prayer stool. You will find more about this in chapter eight on 'Physical spirituality', along with other suggestions.

Accepting God's presence
This is the moment when you move from your preparations and settle into saying in some way or other, 'Here I am, Lord.' It can be a simple statement of your desire, however faint; or even an owning up to not wanting to pray while

still having a willingness to be there. Listening to the sounds around you and then to your own breathing can help, using the rise and fall, the rhythm of in and out, imaginatively to breathe in God's Spirit and his love, and breathe out your anxieties and concerns. God is always with us – that is the very meaning of Jesus' name, 'Immanuel' (Matthew 1:23), but we are not always aware of him. The actual process you are beginning is often called 'centring down', though the words of the psalmist give a better description: 'Be still, and know that I am God' (Psalm 46:10). Try repeating these words slowly in rhythm with your breathing, pausing after every second word: 'Be still . . . and know . . . that I . . . am God'. In this way you can act out your intention to be open to God, and this is valuable in itself, even if you have difficulty in letting your attention focus on him in any of the following ways.

Using a symbol

Some people find a visual focus helpful. The focus could be a lighted candle or a picture or an icon. Watching a flame, whether steady or flickering, can stimulate different reflections on light and darkness, bringing our imagination to life and with it a fresh awareness of a phrase of scripture: 'The light shines in the darkness, and the darkness has not overcome it' (John 1:5, RSV). At first you may find you have reservations about using a symbolic object, particularly if it has associations which you find unhelpful. (Some Christians, for example, would not wish to use a crucifix.) Start with a symbol which attracts you and use others as you feel able.

Less obvious symbols which can provide ways into this kind of praying are a glass of water, a piece of bread, a well-formed stone, a seed pod, an empty bowl held gently before you, or a flower of the field to simply 'consider' as Jesus suggested (Matthew 6:28). Some symbols need to be looked at, others felt (your sense of touch can be part of praying) or just accepted as there with you, assisting you to come to quietness or move into imaginative reflection. Postcards and pictures are an obvious and easily available resource. Over a period of time you may like to collect an album of pictures or images which you find are stepping stones into becoming aware of the presence of God. Your selection could well include prayer cards, postcards of paintings and sculptures, as well as scenes of great beauty in the natural world. However, do not overlook more disturbing pictures showing human conflict or suffering. These can be stepping stones as you search for God's presence in the dark side of life. Whatever way your time of prayer develops, there is value in closing the time with a specific thought or spoken prayer arising out of your awareness, or by thanking God for any new insight.

Repeating a significant word, phrase or simple sentence
Repetition, used rhythmically, can help you move into stillness. It can also help move the centre of your praying from your mind into your heart, or inner self. This is an important movement away from thinking *about* God to being *with* him, and all of the ways of praying that are outlined here encourage this change in awareness. God's Spirit within you wants to help you to say 'Abba, Father' (Galatians 4:6) and, 'Maranatha' – 'Come, O Lord' (1 Corinthians 16:22).

There are many other words, especially names, titles and characteristics of God, which you can use, such as Immanuel, Lamb of God, Jesus, Saviour, or ejaculations like 'Hallelujah! or 'Praise the Lord!' Your special phrases could include 'Peace be with you', 'In the beginning God . . . ', 'The Lord is my light', 'God is love', ' Let not your hearts be troubled', 'Lord, have mercy'. Full sentences are a development of this and can be linked with rhythmic breathing. The Jesus Prayer from the Orthodox Christian tradition is used in this way, breathing in and out steadily whilst saying quietly or repeating in your thoughts, 'Lord Jesus Christ, Son of God, have mercy on me, a sinner.' The well known verse, 'Be still, and know that I am God' (Psalm 46:10), has already been mentioned. Other helpful verses might include the 'I am' sayings of Jesus in John's Gospel, or individual beatitudes from the Sermon on the Mount (Matthew 5:3–12), or the promise, 'I will be with you always' (Matthew 28:20). Any appropriate short sentence from scripture can be used in this way, to still the mind and body and allow your inner self to come to rest in God. Simple worship songs, with few words yet repeated, can be another way into praying using these basic principles.

Relishing scripture
Too much, too quickly, can cause indigestion! There are many ways and reasons for reading scripture. This prayerful approach, stopping to savour what attracts you, is often attributed to the Benedictine tradition of devotion. Instead of attempting to read a whole passage, the secret lies in reading slowly, aloud or in a low whisper, with frequent pauses so that the words are *heard* as well as seen and read. Then when a particular word or phrase resonates, or 'rings a bell' with you, repeat it slowly as many times as you find helpful, savouring its significance for you. This can be a very good way of reading, and so praying, psalms such as:

> Psalm 23, 'The Lord is my shepherd'
> Psalm 51, 'Have mercy on me, O God'
> Psalm 84, 'How lovely is your dwelling-place'
> Psalm 103, 'Praise the Lord, O my soul'
> Psalm 139, 'O Lord, you have searched me'

As well as many other psalms, there are other passages of scripture which can be read in this way, for example Genesis 1, Isaiah 6:1–8, Isaiah 12, 40, 53, 55 and 61, Hosea 11: 1–11, 1 Corinthians 13, Ephesians 1 and 3:14–21. Here you are at the gateway to exploring meditation, which is developed in chapter nine. The slow reading of scripture, savouring what attracts you, is a sure way of receiving God's living word into your inner self in a profoundly personal way, allowing it to become a stimulus to pray 'from the heart'.

Praying great prayers
St Augustine, St Francis, St Ignatius and many other Christians have left us prayers which encapsulate in a concise form our desires and hopes. We learn language by hearing others speak and by imitating them; likewise in learning to pray. Listening to and using good examples, spoken aloud or whis-

pered reflectively, can help you to express yourself in a well ordered way whilst touching deep chords within you. The popularity of the prayer attributed to St Francis, 'Make me an instrument of your peace', illustrates how helpful it is to use the mature prayers of others. Jesus recognised the value of learning such prayers by heart when he gave his disciples what we call the Lord's Prayer as a pattern for them to use each time they prayed (Luke 11:2–4). This chapter includes several great prayers for you to use in this way and there are many good anthologies of prayers that you may find an enriching resource for your devotions. In the same way, Christian hymns read slowly can be a further source for personal prayer. Some were even written as prayers, eg 'Teach me, my God and King' by George Herbert.

Speaking from the heart

All the ways of praying suggested so far encourage a listening disposition, seeking to be attentive and open to God, in seeming contrast to the spontaneous praying which you may express at other times of the day. This is not intended to exclude spontaneous or conversational forms of prayer in your specific times of devotion. Rather these forms of prayer will have a new depth if they arise out of having listened first to God and then having allowed the Spirit of God to help you express your inner self to him and sense his response. You may even find that you are given a personal way of expressing your inner self at times which sounds like another language. This is called speaking in tongues and is mentioned in Paul's first letter to the church in Corinth (1 Corinthians 12:10).

Jesus clearly prayed spontaneously and freely out of a profound and personal knowledge of God his Father. In this way he follows and fulfils the example of many Old Testament writers. The psalmists poured out their souls (Psalm 42:4), groaned and sighed (Psalm 38:8–9), cried out in anguish (Psalm 42:1–3) and complained in their regular times of prayer. They also gave thanks to God, expressed joy and wonder, adoration and praise, as well as dereliction and despair. The whole range of emotional experience and ways of using language are found in their prayers and are just as appropriate when praying today. Sometimes you may come to your time of prayer with an outburst of praise or great personal distress and then 'dry up'. However, most times you will find that you need a settling time in which to collect your thoughts and focus your attention before talking with God in a conversational kind of way, sharing the matters which concern you. This kind of praying can lead naturally into making specific requests and end with an offering of yourself. A final prayer of self-offering is a valuable way of ending, helping you to come to a definite close instead of drifting out of your praying into the activities of the day.

Asking for ourselves and for others

Jesus encouraged his followers to ask (John 14:14; 16:23; Luke 11:9–13 and Matthew 6:8), even though God our Father knows our needs even before we ask him. Simplicity and honesty is therefore the best approach, the point being that through the act of asking you are clarifying your request whilst also expressing your desire and trust. You may find that you have different preferences at different stages of your Christian pilgrimage and the ways of expressing a request can vary from a spoken prayer to a deep sigh of longing. In all asking prayer the Holy Spirit is at work stimulating and interpreting your longings and concerns from deep within (Romans 8:26–27). For this reason the different ways into praying outlined here can bring a new quality of reflection and discernment into your praying. By asking after waiting quietly and listening carefully, your requests can become more in tune with seeking the kingdom of God and desiring to be more conformed to the way of Christ the Lord. It is through this aspect of praying that God invites us to share in his care of creation and our neighbours, as we learn to will his will and ask aright.

Some people find lists of names or topics useful when seeking to pray for others. Perhaps having your diary or calendar with you may help your concentration. Or writing down the names of the people you are concerned about and then offering this to God on the open palms of your hands is a possible approach. These very practical suggestions have their roots in the Old Testament. There you can read of how the high priest wore a breastplate on which were all the names of the tribes of Israel, thereby symbolising being in the presence of God on behalf of others (Exodus 28:29). This is what Jesus is forever doing on our behalf in the presence of God the Father, exposing our needs and disgrace to the Father's almighty love and grace and mercy (Hebrews 7:25).

The late Bishop Michael Ramsey used to describe this kind of intercessory prayer (asking on behalf of others) as simply 'to be with God with the people on your heart'. Some of your concerns may be beyond your capacity to put into words. A scene from a famine, a flood or an act of appalling terrorism, may bring forth few words yet deep emotion. The same experience can happen in personal sorrow or when praying for people whom you love who are very ill. 'To be there before you, Lord, that's all . . . ' is the way Michel Quoist begins one of his *Prayers of Life* (Gill & MacMillan 1965). Your asking may be like that at times, when to be there in anguish is the only kind of prayer you know. Then you can let your concern spill over into the silent and sovereign love of the crucified God. And by his grace you can be there again later on in relief, appreciation and thanksgiving.

So asking is not about pleading with an unresponsive God, but entering into the presence of him who is eternal and is ever working for your good (Romans 8:28).

POSTSCRIPT

A more traditional way of describing prayer is to identify the various elements, for example adoration, confession, thanksgiving and supplication, seeking to provide a structure to work through in each prayer time. By contrast, the approach shown here, by focusing on preparation and ways into praying, allows these elements to arise as the Spirit prompts and attracts. Being in the presence of God, however partially perceived, can lead to any of these elements in any order, stimulated by the symbols, prayers or parts of scripture being used. What matters most is that you seek to become aware of being in relationship with God and let your time with him unfold, moving from your preparations into his presence and from your head into the Spirit in your heart, responding from that deeper level of your inner self.

> To be with God wondering, that is adoration.
> To be with God gratefully, that is thanksgiving.
> To be with God ashamed, that is confession.
> To be with God with others on your heart, that is intercession. *Bishop Michael Ramsey*

More than anything else, prayer, as Clement of Alexandria said, is 'keeping company with God'. The following exercises are to help you do just that.

TAKE SEVEN DAYS . . .

These exercises suggest a regular pattern for you to follow each day for a week. The emphasis is on being quiet and unhurried. Before you start:

> Decide where and when you will pray.
> Think about which body posture you will use.
> Consider whether using a symbol or picture might be helpful. If so, will you use a different one or the same one each day?

Day 1

• A sentence to repeat as you settle:

> 'Be still, and know that I am God.' *Psalm 46:10*

• A psalm to savour: Psalm 34:1–10.

• A silence to keep.

• A reading to reflect on: Luke 4:42.

• A time for personal asking – out loud, by gesture or in silence.

• A prayer to pray:

> Gracious and holy Father, give us wisdom to perceive you, diligence to seek you, patience to wait for you,

eyes to behold you, a heart to meditate on you, and a
life to proclaim you; through the power of the Spirit
of Jesus Christ our Lord.   *St Benedict*

- A time for self-offering:

    Lord Jesus, I give you my hands to do your work.
    I give you my feet to go your way.
    I give you my eyes to see as you do.
    I give you my tongue to speak your words.
    I give you my mind that you may think in me.
    I give you my spirit that you may pray in me.
    Above all, I give you my heart
    that you may love through me
    your Father and all mankind.
    I give you my whole self that you may grow in me,
    so that it is you, Lord Jesus, who live and work and
    pray in me.   *Grail Prayer*

- A blessing to receive:

    May God himself, the God of peace, sanctify you
    through and through. May your whole spirit, soul and
    body be kept blameless at the coming of our Lord
    Jesus Christ.   *1 Thessalonians 5:23*

Day 2

- A sentence to repeat:

    Trust in the Lord for ever, for the Lord, the Lord, is
    the Rock eternal.   *Isaiah 26:4*

- A psalm to savour: Psalm 39:5–9.

- A silence to keep.

- A reading to reflect on: Luke 11:1–4.

- A time for personal asking.

- A prayer to pray:

    Eternal God, the light of the minds that know you,

the joy of the hearts that love you, and the strength of the wills that serve you; grant us so to know you that we may truly love you, and so to love you that we may fully serve you, whom to serve is perfect freedom, in Jesus Christ our Lord.

After St Augustine

• A time for self-offering: how will you offer yourself to God today? In silence? In a simple but very personal sentence? Or through one of the set prayers shown in these pages?

• A blessing to receive:

May our Lord Jesus Christ himself and God our Father, who loved us and by his grace gave us eternal encouragement and good hope, encourage your hearts and strengthen you in every good deed and word.

2 Thessalonians 2:16–17

Day 3

• A sentence to repeat:

... his compassions never fail. They are new every morning; great is your faithfulness.

Lamentations 3:22–23

• A psalm to savour: Psalm 19:1–6.

• A silence to keep.

• A reading to reflect on: Luke 11:5–13.

• A time for personal asking.

• A prayer to pray:

Christ be with me,
Christ within me,
Christ behind me,
Christ before me,
Christ beside me,
Christ to win me,
Christ to comfort and restore me,

Christ beneath me,
Christ above me,
Christ in quiet,
Christ in danger,
Christ in hearts of all that love me,
Christ in mouth of friend or stranger.

> Ascribed to *St Patrick* (tr. Mrs C F Alexander,
> from *St Patrick's Breastplate*)

• A prayer of self-offering: use the Grail Prayer on page 73, offering each part of yourself through it to Jesus and the Father.

• A blessing to receive:

May the Lord direct your hearts into God's love and Christ's perseverance. *2 Thessalonians 3:5*

Day 4

• A sentence to repeat:

Praise be to the God and Father of our Lord Jesus Christ, who has blessed us in the heavenly realms with every spiritual blessing in Christ. *Ephesians 1:3*

• A psalm to savour: Psalm 103:8–18.

• A silence to keep.

• A reading to reflect on: Luke 22:39–46.

• A time for personal asking.

• A prayer to pray:

Thank you, dear Jesus,
for all you have given me,
for all you have taken away from me,
for all you have left me. *Sir Thomas More*

• A time for self-offering: use whatever way of self-offering you find helpful today, whether silent or spoken, with words or gestures.

- A blessing to receive:

> Now may the Lord of peace himself give you peace at all times and in every way. *2 Thessalonians 3:16*

Day 5

- A sentence to repeat:

> The Lord is my shepherd, I shall not want.
> *Psalm 23:1, RSV*

- A psalm to savour: Psalm 37:1–11.

- A silence to keep.

- A reading to reflect on: Luke 23:32–34.

- A time for personal asking.

- A prayer to pray:

> Lord, to be turned from you is to fall, to be turned to you is to rise, and to stand in you is to abide for ever; grant us in all our duties your help, in all our perplexities your guidance, in all our dangers your protection, and in all our sorrows your peace; through Jesus Christ our Lord. *St Augustine*

- A time for self-offering: return to the Grail Prayer (page 73) to offer your whole self to Jesus and the Father.

- A blessing to receive:

> May the God of hope fill you with all joy and peace as you trust in him, so that you may overflow with hope by the power of the Holy Spirit. *Romans 15:13*

Day 6

- A sentence to repeat:

> The light shines in the darkness, and the darkness has not overcome it. *John 1:5, RSV*

- A psalm to savour: Psalm 84.

- A silence to keep.

- A reading to reflect on: Luke 23:44–46.

- A time for personal asking.

- A prayer to pray:

  > Almighty God, in whom we love and move and have our being, you have made us for yourself, so that our hearts are restless until they rest in you; grant us purity of heart and strength of purpose, that no selfish passion may hinder us from knowing your will, no weakness from doing it; but that in your light we may see light clearly, and in your service find our perfect freedom, through Jesus Christ our Lord.
  >
  > *St Augustine*

- A time for self-offering: use your body and hands to express the attitude you feel and the words you want to say, and offer to God what the Spirit prompts within you, either silently or aloud.

- A blessing to receive:

  > May the God of peace, who through the blood of the eternal covenant brought back from the dead our Lord Jesus, that great Shepherd of the sheep, equip you with everything good for doing his will, and may he work in us what is pleasing to him, through Jesus Christ, to whom be glory for ever and ever. Amen.
  >
  > *Hebrews 13:20–21*

Day 7

Follow the pattern of the previous days' exercises, this time selecting the words, prayers and Bible passages you feel are appropriate for you today. Some prayers are given below for you to choose from if you wish.

- Some words to remember as you begin:

  > Create in me a pure heart, O God, and renew a steadfast spirit within me ... The sacrifices of God are a

broken spirit; a broken and contrite heart, O God, you will not despise. *Psalm 51:10,17*

Merciful Father, I confess my common failings as I live alongside other people: my lack of understanding; my lack of forgiveness; my lack of openness; my lack of sensitivity; the times when I am ... too eager to be better than others; too rushed to care; too tired to bother; too lazy to really listen; but too quick to act from motives other than love. Father, forgive me. Enable me to accept and receive your gracious love.

After *St Francis of Assisi*

Lord Jesus Christ, we thank you for all the benefits you have won for us, for all the pains and insults you have borne for us. Most merciful redeemer, friend and brother, may we know you more clearly, love you more dearly and follow you more nearly, day by day. Amen. *St Richard of Chichester*

Come, Lord, day after day.
Come for mankind,
Come for us all,
Come for me.

Roger Schultz, Taizé

5

PRAYING TOGETHER

Roger Pooley

Prayer is personal. As John Bunyan put it, it is 'our most direct and immediate personal approach into the presence of God'. Jesus warned his disciples about praying in public simply to be seen and admired, but that doesn't mean we must only pray on our own. Jesus' model prayer begins, '*Our* Father . . . ', which reminds us that our prayer joins with that of our fellow Christians, whether they are in the same building or not. Jesus promised that when two or three gathered together in prayer, he would be there, ready to act (Matthew 18:19–20); and, in the moment of agony in Gethsemane, he rebuked his disciples for not being able to support him by praying with him (Matthew 26:40).

However, the disciples, though they were stumblers like us, were good learners. One of the marks of the church in Acts – before, during and after Pentecost – was its praying together, whether in members' homes or as part of the temple worship. Any group of Christians who want to grow – whether it's a church or a Christian Union or just a bunch of friends – will desire to get back to the vitality and power of the fellowship of the early church. And so, following that example, they will seek to grow in their prayer life together.

LEARNING TO PRAY WITH OTHERS
So how do you start? Many Christians will have first experienced group prayer in the same way I did when, as a teenager,

I started going to the Bible study and prayer meeting in the back room of the church. After someone had led a Bible study, or we had heard a visiting speaker expound a passage, we would 'pray round' the circle of the dozen or so who had turned up, after first discussing who or what we would pray for. After we had learnt the language considered appropriate for prayers in this gathering, my friend and I were always happiest when we were at the start of the circle because there were so many topics to choose from. We dreaded coming after a man we nicknamed 'Rambling Rose' because he would pray for everything on the list and leave us with only a few pathetic supplementary petitions to make. If only I had known how encouraging it is to hear a new Christian stumble out their first public prayers, I wouldn't have been so embarrassed. I can look back and laugh at my adolescent nerves, but I look back in gratitude for what those meetings taught me. I learnt to lift my horizons and expectations of prayer. I also began to realise that when God wants to make his presence felt in a group, he often does it when they are praying together. I can remember one time when we were praying in no set order and nobody wanted to stop. The usual fifteen minutes spread to nearly an hour. Looking back, that was a turning point in the life of our church; the Spirit had decided to blow, just as he did at Pentecost.

These days many churches have decentralised their prayer meetings and they are part of a house-group structure. This can make for a more relaxed and experimental approach to prayer, though it does have the disadvantage that the church as a whole doesn't have the same experience of praying together. It may need to compensate by having an occasional (monthly?) time together, or by setting aside special times at particular moments of decision-making. Some version of the prayer vigil might be appropriate on such occasions. A whole evening, or a Saturday, could be set aside for prayer, but the time would be split up into hour or half-hour sections so that people could come and go as their commitments permitted. There might be different leaders for the sections, and these sections might emphasise different aspects of prayer or ways of praying together. It shouldn't become an endurance test!

However group prayer is structured into church life – and it can be as part of a low profile house group or as an all night extravaganza – we are faced with a second challenge: making it work.

MAKING IT WORK

Leadership
In the Christian way of doing things, leadership is a matter of service rather than lording it over others (Matthew 20:26–28). Leading a time of prayer means enabling people to pray, not inhibiting them from doing so. It means finding ways of involving people without putting them on the spot – though a little tactful coaxing can help growth! The leader needs to be clear about what's going on. There is a balance between structuring the prayer time so that, for instance, the various elements of prayer – worship, confession, asking for things, and so on – get proper weight, and using 'being open to the Spirit' as an excuse for chaos. It might mean doing some tactful talking behind the scenes, so that the inexperienced learn to pray and the stiflingly voluble hold back.

The leader may be responsible for seeing that prayers are led, but it doesn't mean he or she has to lead every time. Volunteers may be asked for, or each person present might lead in turn. This can be particularly helpful in the kind of group where there are different traditions represented; that way the group benefits from its variety as well as its unity.

Leaders may also need to rebuke members, sometimes. For instance, group prayer can be used to accuse someone in the group: 'Please help Mavis control her temper', when Mavis is sitting in the same room without having asked for that help! Or it may be used for gossip, breaching a confidence or an intimacy under the cloak of prayer. Generally a group will grow together in what its members feel they can share, but presuming on that level of intimacy can be destructive and a backward step. A quiet word in private is often all that is needed.

What words shall we use?

A common model is *extempore* prayer, in which words are thought of on the spot. It has the great virtue of flexibility, fitting the moment, the mood, the need precisely. If someone asks us to pray for them, we can immediately turn that request into a prayer to God with the minimum of fuss. From another perspective, its immediacy can give scope to the Holy Spirit to inspire our words, if we are being attentive to God as well as our own needs. The conversational style is also very suitable to the smaller group which is, after all, friends talking to their heavenly Father. Yet there can be the tendency to get stuck in jargon, or a small repertoire of key phrases. This results in the group having all the disadvantages of using set prayers without the advantages!

What about *written* prayers? It may be useful, not just for variety, to use a sequence of written prayers, whether from one of the denominational prayer books or from one of the many compilations that are available. There is sometimes a richness and precision of phrasing here that can elude extempore prayer. It can also mean that the silence between prayers is not fraught with the anxiety about who is going to pray next. One form of written prayer that I find particularly useful for groups is the litany which includes a regular response, like 'Hear our prayer' to 'Lord in your mercy . . . ' There are some useful and fresh ones in the Taizé booklet *Praying Together*. You can also make up your own. A group meeting in the evening might sometimes enjoy using an evening service of prayer, like one of the modern versions of compline which was originally a monastic office.

Groups also have a collective memory for set words. The most valuable is the Lord's Prayer which can be used as a summary at the end of a time of more open prayer, or as a structure for prayer, with silent or spoken meditation on each phrase. The grace (2 Corinthians 13:14) can also helpfully be said together. Again, slowing it down is one way of ensuring that familiar words don't lose their meaning. Choruses, worship songs, even verses from hymns, sung or said, can help in making worship a central part of praying.

SOME GUIDELINES FOR EXTEMPORE PRAYER

- Addressing God. The name we use for God is important. The Bible is full of different names for him so don't feel he always has to be 'Dear Lord and Heavenly Father'. You might begin a prayer which appeals to God's love, for example 'Loving Lord Jesus'. A prayer which appeals to God's sovereignty might begin 'Almighty God, you create and sustain everything . . . '

- Pray don't preach. You are praying on behalf of the group, not sneaking in a rebuke to them.

- Use real English. God understands ordinary words and is unimpressed by religious rhetoric. It will also help you and the group to be clear what you are asking for.

- Stick to the point. Rambling prayers are like badly packed suitcases – it's hard to tell what they contain. And such prayers are difficult to say 'Amen' to. If the group is praying to an agreed agenda, leave topics for others to bring up.

- Don't be afraid of quiet. Don't just pray because no one else is. Try to be sensitive to the prompting of the Spirit. If you are summing up in prayer at the end of a meeting, or you are the only person praying in a service, leave some space for quiet reflection or private petition.

- Stop. Conclude with some such phrase as 'in Jesus' name, Amen' so people know when you have stopped and can add their assent (even in a group where 'Amens' and 'Yes Lords' are common in the middle of prayers).

The familiarity of words may be a hindrance – they can be recited without engaging the head or the heart – but equally they can release us from searching for words, so we can concentrate our attention on the depths beneath those words.

Silence together
At first sight it may seem odd to gather together for prayer and then to pray completely in silence; but it can be a major step forward for a group to use silence as part or all of its prayer time.

A silence which is used as punctuation between words can be a useful start. It can allow space for reflection on words that have been spoken. It can help introduce an element of awe into worship: a sense that God's greatness may be expressed in words but also stops our mouth. A time of silence may be used to allow people to pray silently for matters that cannot be shared fully with the group, or where there isn't enough information to pray intelligently. This isn't second-best, it's just the way things often are.

'Julian groups' are groups that meet for silent prayer. They are named after Julian of Norwich, a medieval mystic. The host or leader of such a group may often introduce the time of quiet with a reading or, perhaps, some music. In the early days of the group there may be some instruction on how to use the silence. Then the group will be silent together for an agreed length of time (which may be quite short to begin with). The emphasis is on listening to God, perhaps meditating on the reading to start with, or thinking of the needs of the world. However, it is not just about saying prayers in silence, doing under one's breath what would usually be done aloud. For some, silence is oppressive, even searching. For others, it may be precisely what they need, a gift from God in a noisy and verbose existence.

> There was a lovely silence in the Brethren assembled on Sunday morning as we waited for the Spirit. Either the Spirit was moving someone to speak who was taking his sweet time or else the Spirit was playing a

> wonderful joke on us and letting us sit, or perhaps
> silence was the point of it.   *Garrison Keillor*

Praying together in the silence is different from doing it alone.
Apart from the discipline and the freedom from interruption
which is often difficult for the solitary pray-er, there is a sense
that the group is listening together to God. It might then
be that such times of praying together in silence could be
useful as part of the strategy for a group or a church looking
for guidance or direction.

What you do after the silence is important. People must
be given time to come out of it slowly if it has been at all
lengthy. The Society of Friends (Quakers) speak of talking
out of the silence, sharing words and ideas which have come
from the time of silent waiting on God. There may need to
be a space for informal sharing before chatter sets in.

Praying for each other

The prayer time will often focus on the needs of the group.
A church prayer meeting will want to pray for its minister,
its Sunday school and so on. A missionary prayer meeting
may be set up for the express purpose of praying for a particular country or society. A prayer group mustn't get too inward-
looking or it will fall short of its Master's prayer; but it is
important to be able to share personal concerns. How can
we do this most effectively?

Every prayer group I have been a member of has had a
different level of 'permission' of what we can ask prayer for.
It's important to make this as wide as the group's trust will
allow. Try not to get stuck in praying only about 'religious'
concerns, like a talk you have to give, or a youth club you
are responsible for; and not just about personal crises, like a
death in the family, or an exam to be sat.

The leader may ask for prayer requests from individuals,
and these may accumulate until the time for prayer begins.
(Be careful that the asking time doesn't exceed the prayer
time.) At a group I was once part of, after each request the
leader asked someone to lead the group in prayer for that
individual, while those around the person prayed for would

A PATTERN FOR A PRAYER MEETING

Arrival Time. Allow 15 minutes for introductions, chat and relaxing into the group.

Worship. Read a psalm together (agree on a version, or have copies), or sing a couple of worship songs, or listen to a recording of some music. The leader may want to add a prayer of thanks for the day and lead the group in quiet confession, reminding them of God's forgiveness.

Activity. In many groups, where Bible study and prayer is combined, this may be the time to study. But be open to other ways for the group to be stimulated into prayer and action. Use a Bible passage for guided meditation, for example, entering into prayer through the thoughts and questions of the disciples in a Gospel story, or of Abraham or Moses faced with a call from God. A sequence of slides or an excerpt from a tape may inform or help meditation, though the leader will have to think of ways of helping the group to be active in response. Bring out the creative gifts in the group – such as photography, music or writing – to make your own audio-visual aids.

Prayer time. Try to have a routine pattern, which is occasionally broken by a fresh way of doing things. Having a different leader each week may provide enough variety. Prayer times should usually involve sharing of, and prayer for, the needs of group members and those close to them. Don't forget to look beyond the group and pray for the needs of the wider church and world.

Close by saying the Lord's Prayer or the Grace slowly together.

lay their hands on him or her as a physical sign of support. I found this very helpful when I was prayed for, though there was an embarrassment barrier to be crossed.

This kind of prayer for one another can be done silently using a symbol, for example a lighted candle which is passed from one person to the next. While you are holding the candle, the group prays for you, offering you in the quiet to the 'light of the world'. A rough agreement on timing may be needed or the leader can do the clock-watching for everyone. This can work surprisingly well in groups which don't really know each other or who have members who are reticent. You have to pray with your eyes open, of course!

Another group I know will ask one or two people each week to talk in some depth about themselves as a starter for prayer. However, they are not asked for formal 'items for payer'. Rather, they might explain what their job is, who they work with, what the particular goals, stresses and joys of the job are, and so on. Or they might say what their day is like (they don't have to be employed to answer this one), talk about the people they meet or have a lot to do with, and so on. This helps the group to pray for each other with depth and fullness.

Praying for others

There are times when outside needs are obvious – someone we know is ill, the results of an earthquake are shown on the television news, and so on. However, our knowledge, and concern, often need to be stimulated. Many missionary societies and relief agencies produce materials suitable for groups, using cassettes, slides or videos, which can lead to informed prayer. The group does not have to be full of international relations experts to pray for peace, but prayer and knowledge are linked. A group may pray better if they are linked with a particular person or place by regular correspondence and giving.

Troubleshooting

Some people find it difficult to pray out loud in a group. Here are some suggestions to help them speak out their prayers.

Encourage the 'agreement prayer', one which doesn't look for a new topic but agrees with and builds on the previous one.

Ask everyone in the group to confine themselves to intercessions of one sentence or even one name.

Allot topics to people in the group and give them time to write down their prayers; or ask them to take a special responsibility for a particular situation and get them to bring information for prayer to the group every so often.

Share out local and national newspapers and get everyone to circle stories or individuals that need prayer.

FAMILY PRAYERS

Praying together should be a feature of every Christian group. So far we have looked at church groups, but another (and most important) group which can meet for prayer is the family. Some people have a mental caricature of the Victorian family at prayer, children and servants meeting twice a day to be spiritually browbeaten by the master of the house. Actually, if you look at some of the old manuals of family prayers, they are very simple, consisting of a short scripture reading one or two prayers and the Lord's Prayer. The old understanding that the father is the 'bishop' of the family did sometimes make for a sense of oppression; but William Wilberforce, a leader of the evangelical revival in the early nineteenth century which stressed family prayers, was also concerned that children should not be 'overdosed with religion'. So, how can a family pray effectively and meaningfully together?

One simple way is to say grace before meals. A family which has breakfast on the run and lunch in five different places may find it difficult, but Sunday lunch or an evening meal together may be a good time to thank God together for all his blessings. With children, or at a special celebration, try using music, singing a simple chorus or doxology (eg 'Praise God from whom all blessings flow'). Holding hands around the table can add a special touch.

As with personal private prayer, it is best to set a target

that can be met each week or most days rather than being hopelessly ambitious and giving up early, or feeling permanently guilty. A simple pattern of a brief reading from the Bible (or, occasionally, some other devotional material), prayers of worship, thanks and confession, followed by requests for help for the family and its friends, and the Lord's Prayer, is ample. It is important for every member of the family to be, and feel, involved, and to feel free rather than browbeaten about it, especially if there are tensions and upsets. We need to show children that prayer is important, and that it changes things; but we don't want to give them such a heavy, unpleasant dose that they will be inoculated against prayer for life.

Prayer need not always involve the whole family; children at different ages have different capacities and need one-to-one help. And the praying need not be all one way: the son who prays about his father's interview is doing as important a job as the father praying for his son's bad knee.

Those who are married may find that praying with one's partner can be wonderfully helpful, but surprisingly difficult. Many Christian couples I know find it hard to pray together with any regularity; others have regular times daily or weekly or will set aside extended times to pray, for instance to ask for God's guidance when there is a hard and momentous decision to be made. If starting is difficult, start very simply. Use the Lord's Prayer, each saying alternate phrases while looking at each other or holding hands.

In all these modes of praying together, there has to be an element of routine or there won't be much regularity. But equally, there have to be ways of breaking the routine, of being creative. Use different sources for words and different postures. The arrival of babies, or children growing up, may disrupt the routine and odd moments of peace may be all that's available, but it is important to keep going.

PRAYER PARTNERS AND TRIPLETS

Some of my most precious experiences in prayer have been with just one other person. These have come out of various schemes. When I was a student our college Christian Union divided into different pairs each term and each pair met once a week for a cup of tea and spent half an hour praying over personal concerns and those of friends and families. Why was it so good? I suppose there was a level of sharing which would have been inappropriate in a larger group. In particular, we tended to feel much easier about confessing our doubts and weaknesses with just one other person. And we didn't have to be good at prayer.

A further variation on the 'prayer partners' idea is the 'prayer triplet', which is often used to get people in a neighbourhood praying in preparation for mission, but which has wider possibilities. In its simplest form it involves three people agreeing to pray together regularly, each bringing the names of three people who are not Christians (friends, family, workmates, etc) to the group for prayer. So the group is praying for nine people, perhaps with the idea of inviting them to an evangelistic event, or that they become Christians in some other way. (A helpful book is *Three Times Three Equals Twelve* by Brian Mills.) Obviously the idea is extendable and can be based in a workplace or school. Its virtue is its simple directness. It can be very effective, not just because of the prayer, but because of the encouragement derived from knowing that you are not the only person praying, and that you have the support of others as you witness.

Finally, there is great virtue in praying with friends, as and when it seems appropriate. Recently a Christian couple I know, who were having a hard time, asked me to pray for them and to ask anyone else I knew and had confidence in to pray, too. I phoned another Christian friend and told him; and he and his wife immediately asked me round that Sunday evening so that we could pray together. I had not expected such an immediate response, but it seemed so right and helpful. There doesn't have to be a prayer meeting arranged for a group of Christian friends, or just two or three of them, to get together for prayer. There doesn't have to be an air of 'put-on piety' about it either. Just sitting down and doing it may be better than the promise that 'I'll pray for you' which so often isn't kept.

Setting up a prayer partners or triplets scheme

In a church or Christian Union group the idea needs to be introduced, a list put up (already 'seeded' with some willing volunteers), then people put together in a thoughtful way. Suggest how regularly the partners should meet – weekly or fortnightly. All that is needed then is a quiet room for no more than an hour. The partners need to talk for a while, to get to know each other and to admit honestly their apprehensions and expectations. Then they have to plunge in! Set a simple agenda for prayer: thanks and praise to God, each other's needs, families and friends, people who aren't Christians. The atmosphere and desire to pray is more important than the fluency of the words. Then the next time, begin by sharing answers to prayer or developments in the situation, so that trust in God and in each other can grow. Depending on the size of the scheme, there should be a change-round and an opportunity to opt in and out every month or two.

TAKE SEVEN DAYS . . .

In keeping with the theme of this chapter, the following material is especially for use in a group situation. Each day's exercise focuses on prayers of the apostle Paul. As Donald Coggan points out in his book, *Prayers of the New Testament*, Paul didn't give the young churches he addressed in his letters his theory of prayer; he shared his experiences of prayer, and exhorted them to pray.

Day 1

• Read Romans 15:5–6. The key phrase is in verse 5: 'God, who gives endurance and encouragement'. The context is the duties that Christian people have to each other. In chapter 14 Paul has been expanding on Jesus' teaching about not judging one another. At the beginning of chapter 15 he tells the Romans to help the weak by living so as to help others rather than please themselves. A judgmental attitude (which means we despise those whom we consider weak rather than helping them) can undermine a church very quickly. Patient endurance and mutual encouragement are essential, and they come from having a Christ-like attitude: taking the insults, not being sensitive about status. In verse 13 Paul prays that the Romans may grow in the power of the Spirit; the quiet, healing virtues of endurance and encouragement need the more powerful impetus of the hope that Christ will continue to fulfil all God's promises.

• Imagine yourself in the two roles of the Pharisee and the tax collector about whom Jesus told the story recorded in Luke 18:9–14. Start by being the Pharisee. Imagine the sort of self-satisfied prayer that lurks in your own attitudes. Shock yourself with your arrogance. Then try to imagine yourself praying in the place of the tax collector, recognising your need of God's mercy and the privilege you have of being in God's church.

By yourself, or in your group, consider/talk through the results of this imaginative exercise.

> What did it feel like to be the Pharisee or tax collector?
> Are there superior and judgmental attitudes within us which can undermine our group prayer?
> Pray, asking God's forgiveness where necessary and seeking to encourage others, perhaps using the words of Romans 15:5–6.

Day 2

• Read 1 Corinthians 1:3–9. This prayer is an interesting mixture of petition, thanks and worship. Each element involves recognising that the fellowship the Corinthian Christians had – and the fellowship we have – is created by God. When we pray, we are asking him to cement something he has called us to have with his Son.

• Thank God for each other. If you are using these exercises in a group, pass round a bowl, as a reminder that we are vessels of God's Spirit. Thank God, in silence for a set time, for each person as they hold the bowl. If you are alone, focus on two older Christians who have been a help to you, and two younger Christians whose faith has encouraged you.

Day 3

• Read 2 Corinthians 1:2–5; 13:14. Paul's opening prayer is, perhaps, a hint that all was not well with the relationships in the Corinthian church, and there was a hurt to be healed between them and Paul. He steers clear of using prayer as an accusation – an understandable misuse of prayer that Christians can sometimes get into when they feel hard done by. Instead, he gives us a fine example of the kind of prayer that gains its depth and encouraging quality from its insight into the nature of God. In this prayer Paul thanks God as 'the Father of compassion and the God of all comfort' and recognises that mercy and care, once received, can be passed on for the benefit of the whole church.

• Remember what the disciples of Jesus were like. Look at the miscellaneous bunch around you in church next Sunday! Or in your prayer group! As you do, you will see something of the creativity of the Spirit in holding Christians together. Let the words of 1 Corinthians 13:13 inspire you to pray for one another. You may find it helpful to say this verse together out loud. Say it slowly, with eyes open, looking to one another. Joining hands can be a physical symbol, reinforcing your prayers for each other.

Day 4

• Read Ephesians 3:14–21. This prayer begins in dramatic fashion, intense and worshipful. As verse 15 reminds us, the context is Paul's discovery that the gospel is for everyone, not just for a privileged race. The little groups in Asia Minor that he was addressing shared a great and comprehensive God. Verses 16–19 comprise one sentence bursting with excitement. In a sense Paul is simply praying for strength for them, but his prayer for the church is full of detail about *how* we grow into maturity as well as the grace of God, which is the source of all growth and strength.

Verse 20 is an indication that while our prayers may be stumbling and limited, God's answers are not limited by those prayers. When he gives to us, there is no niggling. There can be no messing, no paddling in the shallows after a prayer like this. It springs from a great sense of the greatness of God; but it implies that his effect on us must be staggering too.

• Recognise how limited your prayers for your church or group are. Now try to apply the daring of Paul's prayer to your specific situation.

Try to write a prayer that will be an application of Paul's prayer to your community. Or you might like to rewrite Ephesians 3:14–21 in your own words and use this as a prayer for your group.

> Go ahead and stumble in your prayers, go ahead and cry. Out of your very weakness your brother is made strong. Out of your own weakness you are made strong by Christ. Out of the inadequacy of your prayer, the inability to express yourself, the shame of your tears, and the urgency of your need, you meet the Saviour who understands you. You are comforted and your brother is strengthened. Out of this weakness your brother, hearing and observing that you are in no better state than he, becomes strong. He is encouraged by your so-called failures that he, too, may meet the Lord in his weakness.   *Rosalind Rinker*

Day 5

• Read Philippians 1:2–11. Paul was writing this letter to those who were close to him. In verses 7 and 8 his joy is linked to a kind of love which is special to Christians because it comes from Christ. Christian prayer for each other is in the language of a loving family – brothers and sisters praying to their Father – through their loving elder brother. Notice that Paul's public prayer arose out of regular private praying, rather than being put on for the occasion. It is Christian love which best grows into knowledge and insight, unlike blind Cupid's love which is likely to fade with more knowledge.

• Pray this prayer (Philippians 1:2–11), rephrasing it, per-haps, for a recently converted Christian, or for the group or church to which you belong. Alternatively, you may wish to use each phrase of the prayer as a springboard into more detailed prayer as appropriate to the particular needs of your group.

Day 6

• Read Colossians 1:9–12. The Colossians weren't Paul's converts, unlike the Ephesians. Look at Colossians 4:12 to see the prayer of one of their evangelists for them. But that didn't prevent Paul from having an intelligent, loving prayerful concern for them. Nor should our prayers for Christians be confined by our circle of acquaintance.

There is a lovely poem in Irina Ratushinskya's *Pencil Letter* where she recognises the warmth on a bitter winter's night in prison as coming from the prayers of those, known and unknown, who cared for her.

Paul's prayer was for knowledge, the kind that we would call wisdom rather than cleverness. It results, as Proverbs teaches us, from the fear of God (the recognition of who God is), not necessarily from education. The purpose of this 'wisdom' is to grow in doing good, to be fruitful as it is often described in the New Testament, and to know God. 'Wisdom' isn't an end in itself.

Paul also prayed for endurance – a quality the church needed under persecution, but equally necessary under the pressures of material prosperity, creeping immorality and selfishness with which our culture (although not appearing to persecute it) is bombarding the church.

• Think about endurance training in prayer. How can we remind ourselves to keep praying for particular people and situations? Here are some suggestions:

Ask one group member to be responsible for reminding the group to pray regularly for a particular person or situation.

Start a prayer diary.

Assemble photos of those you should pray for regularly, and keep them together as a reminder and stimulus.

Brainstorm with your group on other practical ideas which will help you 'devote yourselves to prayer' (Colossians 4:2).

Day 7

• Read 2 Thessalonians 1:2–3,11–12; 2:13–14; 3:1–2. Consider the variety of these passages and write down:

What Paul thanks God for in the Thessalonian church
What qualities he prays that God will develop in them
What he asks them to pray for

Consider how these passages can inform and direct your relationships with one another, and with those outside your group. How will you turn this into prayer?

6

DEVOTION IN THE DARK

Philip Seddon

Christians believe that God is good – even that God is the definition of what goodness is. Christians believe that God is love. However, just as belief in God has been destroyed for many Jews by the Holocaust, so 'earthquake' questions can arise for everyone, Christians included.

EARTHQUAKE QUESTIONS
Imagine:

> Your child is killed in the road in front of your house.
> Your wife/husband dies before your first wedding anniversary.
> You are struck down by a wasting bone disease.
> A mother's only son commits suicide.

Such 'life-and-death' events always raise the same questions:

> 'How could God do this to me?'
> 'How do you expect me to believe God cares any more?'
> 'Is it worth believing?'
> 'Why has this happened?'
> 'Why does God have to get back at me all the time?'

And the emotions experienced are common to all human beings: anger, violence, fury, hopelessness, incomprehension, despair, and varying degrees of mental, physical or spiritual collapse or restructuring. What's it all about?

It is in and through such dark periods that faith can be born, strengthened or abandoned. In periods of crisis we grow or become stunted, spiritually and emotionally; we mature or wither as people and as believers; we are recreated by compassion or destroyed by bitterness. But what about those questions? There's not space to deal with them all in detail, but here are a few 'ways in'.

Look at what the statements assume and expect about ourselves

'I don't deserve this.'

'I deserve better than this.'

'I was right. Faith isn't worth it, in the end.'

'Why has it happened to me? I've never done anyone any harm.'

'God has no right to treat me like this when I've followed him for so long.'

The assumption is that ordinary, 'bad' people might deserve to get punished; but 'I'm not one of those'. When we listen to ourselves saying such things, we can detect the indignation, hurt pride or self-pity – the fruits of self-righteousness – that add to the pain of any event.

Look at what the statements assume and expect about God

'God will always get back at me in some way.'

'I knew it wasn't really worth bothering anyway.'

We can shout at God but, having done so, let us hear the underlying meaning of what we are saying: we believe that God is arbitrary and malicious and dedicated to vengeance and punishment. Then we can turn our hurt, angry feelings into confession of ignorance, prayer for forgiveness and an exploration of the conviction that 'God is love', which nothing can deny. We can also allow God to address us, and allow ourselves to be silent. It is through this interplay of experience and certainty that – crazily and incredibly – faith is strengthened, even if it often feels as though it has been weakened.

Look to others who have experienced darkness before us
This is why so many people in darkness are helped by reading
the book of Job. He refused to accept that his suffering
was any kind of punishment from God. However much his
'friends' counselled him to consider what sin he might have
committed unwittingly, he refused to compromise his integrity,
and refused to believe that their 'tit-for-tat' God was
worth believing in. A petty God who was only interested in
catching people out was no God. He wanted to get to grips
with the real God, despite the fact that God seemed to be his
sworn enemy and seemed to desire his death. Job appealed
to the God who was *really* God in face of the God who only
seemed to be God. This is faith in action.

Look closely to see who, or what, you are really worshipping
Whenever we can catch breath, we need to see who or what
we are in fact worshipping and following, and we need to
choose between god and God, between truth and lie, between
idol and reality, between masochism and freedom. 'Unmasking
the idols' in this way is always important, but especially
so in darkness. A few are able to do this on their own. Most
people need help and guidance when the way is dark, because
things are too confused. When you're not certain whether
you're going out of your mind or not, when you feel that
nobody can ever have experienced such anguish before, when
you feel that nobody could possibly understand your despair
– that's when you need to talk with someone who is already
a companion in the fellowship of suffering and has been
hallowed by the presence of Christ in it.

WHO IS GOD?
This is the question raised right at the beginning of the Bible,
in Genesis 3. The serpent offers Eve the opportunity of possessing
the secret of all wisdom and knowledge and so of
being like God. In Jesus' temptation (recorded in Matthew
4:1–11 and Luke 4:1–13) he was faced with a similar choice
before beginning his ministry. If he would only acknowledge
the direction of the devil, he would be given universal authority
at a stroke.

The question 'Who is God?' comes up again and again in the theology and philosophy of the last two hundred years. Humanity has been invited to displace the supposed idol of God and install itself as the 'lord of the universe'. On an individual level I can be tempted to want to be God, and to arrange the universe around myself and my desires. Those in any form of Christian ministry can begin to think that, if they had a bit more power, things would be in better shape. However, because thinking like this is almost literally 'diabolical', the truth only surfaces when we have been thrown into some kind of confusion or darkness and forced to admit to ourselves that a fundamental misapprehension of who God is underlies our superficial niceness. Then a crisis can be fruitful and a potential breakdown become a breakthrough.

Power – human and divine

Prayer is engagement with God. As we are drawn deeper into God, we may be drawn into deeper waters of prayer. We will discover that prayer is not just happy thoughts on a sunny Saturday afternoon; it is also the most profound confrontation with the forces of darkness and light, within and without. The question of who we really want to be God – God or ourselves – is bound to arise. And the struggle in our prayer life may well be fierce, especially if we have been used to being in charge of things.

This prayer struggle is the key to much growth because it centres on the vital issues of power and control. Power and control are much prized in our culture – and yet they are the very features of our self-determination that God asks us to surrender in order to be able to abandon ourselves to his power, direction and lordship. If he is Lord, we cannot be. Although we would wish our spiritual growth to be painless, this is not possible. Particularly in these areas of letting God be God and of power and control, God typically allows or brings about an experience of darkness – a painful experience – through which new light can dawn.

Here are some examples of experiences of darkness which can throw into sharp focus the question of what is really true – and hence, in the end, of who is God. They all illustrate that points of crisis can, if we let God in, become points of growth.

• Society at large (including, to some degree, the Christian church) places such a high premium on healthy living and muscular or slim bodies that sudden illness throws the whole value-system into confusion. The experience of physical handicap – with all the tensions that brings as the disabled are marginalised in a pseudo-civilised society – shows up the bankruptcy of making health our god.

• An unplanned pregnancy can be seen as a disastrous interruption or an 'accident' to be controlled or dealt with by abortion. Or it can be received as an invitation to hand over control to God, even with all its difficulties, and acknowledge his Lordship.

• Death, the ultimate loss of control, has become – even for many Christians – The Great Defeat. Those who have not learnt to include their death in their lives are those who have not learnt to hand over control of their lives into the hand and power of God.

We often say to ourselves, 'One day, I'll get it all sorted out.' Of course this is pure illusion. Nonetheless, we visualise it as the day of great relaxation, when we are fully and finally in control of our destiny and able to sit back without any thought of trust in the Father. We have to learn that we cannot control God. We would like to have done with the questions 'Why?' and 'How long?' But just as we never finish with the unanswered questions and the challenges of the daily future, so we will never finish with the need for faith, hope and love.

WHO AM I?

This is a question that has become central for 'modern man'. Having abandoned any religious or spiritual framework, he lives in a world where his only ultimate relationship is with himself. But, just as the non-Christian can only define himself in terms of himself, so the Christian can only define himself in terms of Christ's self: human and divine. It is when crisis shatters the illusion that we can be self-sufficient, that we may become more open to the full wonder of what God has done in the incarnation. Because he bridges time and eternity, because he joins the limitedness of human life with the limitlessness of God, we have in Jesus the one who has entered into and can deal with what appears to be the futility of human life. Sometimes, however, we refrain from receiving God's gift in its fullness until all other gifts have crumbled away.

At a purely human level it is stating the obvious to say that people are complex. Add together the animal functions, the biological-electrical-chemical complexity, the world of the senses, the sociological groupings, and then consider these alongside the uniqueness of each of six billion other human beings, and still we have hardly begun. Consider the potential for love, contemplation, hatred, tenderness, destruction, beauty and madness, and we are only on the outskirts of ourselves. Entering in, we realise that it is only as we are challenged, stretched and extended that we grow spiritually; but equally, it is only as we are assaulted, assailed and ignored or hurt by others that we know what it is like not to be needed, wanted, valued, appreciated and desired. When we have ceased to know who we really are, or when events seem to be destroying the last remnants of what gave order and meaning to life – that may be the moment we need to recognise that we are too complex for self-understanding. That may be the moment at which Christ bursts through all our defences in order to make himself known, when we, for the first time, are made to reckon with the living God we had longed for but never dared hope for. We may have to let go the last prop and trust that God will hold us, so that it will be apparent that he both made us and loves us.

LANDMARKS IN THE DARK

When things feel very dark, when your compass seems to have stopped working and your map no longer seems to make any sense, when fog descends – all you can do is stop and wait it out. In mountain guidebooks you sometimes read the instruction: 'Do not attempt to descend by this route in fog'.

Darkness, of whatever kind, usually forces us to stop. Sometimes it is wise to *choose* to stop and assess our bearings. Part of this process is looking to see where we have come from. We need to do this in our spiritual lives. Here are some suggestions on how to start.

• Recite your baptismal promises out loud. For example, 'Do you turn to Christ?' 'I turn to Christ'; 'Do you renounce evil?' 'I renounce evil'; and so on. Use words which are familiar to you from the way in which baptism is administered within your own Christian tradition.

• Say the Lord's Prayer (really the disciples' prayer!) or the 'real' Lord's Prayer ('Abba, Father'), the Creed, or the Jesus Prayer ('Lord Jesus Christ, Son of God, have mercy upon me, a sinner') out loud slowly.

• Sing a favourite hymn of strong faith, such as: 'Oh, the deep, deep love of Jesus'; 'All my hope on God is founded'; 'A safe stronghold our God is still'; or 'O Thou who camest from above'.

• Think back to the cross, the beginning of all our Christian experience. You may find it helpful to handle a physical, perhaps wooden, cross or to make the sign of the cross on your forehead or the front of your body.

• If you have some sense of evil, however vague and uncertain:

Take the authority of Jesus Christ ('By the authority given to me as a disciple of Jesus Christ,' or 'In the name of Jesus').

Make the sign of the cross in front of you, if you find this helpful, and dismiss the negative presence. ('Go to your own place and do not return. You have no business here.')

Ask for help. No Christian can be Superman or Superwoman.

• Proclaim Christ's presence with you, or claim protection

of the Spirit in the name of – that is, in the power of – the Trinity. ('In the name of the Father, and of the Son, and of the Holy Spirit . . . ')

• Put on the whole armour of God in your imagination in prayer (Ephesians 6:10–18).

• Remember: 'I am not alone in this darkness. I am in Christ, who is here. He is my salvation. In him I am in the company of all who have fought and won. I can stand in him. Even if I am afraid, there is one Lord: Jesus Christ. Not all the power of hell can shake his kingdom.'

• Laugh at Satan. This was Luther's advice. For him, seriousness was the face of the devil!

• Above all, live in the fact – if not in the feelings – of the crucifixion and the resurrection of Christ: his desolation and triumph on the cross, and his descent into and victory over the powers of darkness.

GROUND TO STAND ON

During an experience of darkness many things are shaken, 'so that what cannot be shaken may remain' (Hebrews 12:27). The house built on the sandy ground of a nominal assent to Christ collapses; the house built on the rock of obedience to Christ (just! – it seems at times) survives.

For the Christian the Bible points us to the Rock of Christ on which to build. Verses of scripture can provide 'ground to stand on' during times of darkness. Not every verse fits every situation in life, but those listed below have nourished believers through rough and difficult times. They can be turned over in the mind, chewed over, and sent down to the stomach for further 'inward digestion'.

Sometimes you can enter more deeply into the meaning of a text by turning it upside down or back to front. Or turn positive to negative to see what it yields. Or try emphasising each word of the text in turn. However, don't use scripture as a sledgehammer to smash yourself with. Rather use it as a key to open doors.

'Surely the Lord is in this place, and I was not aware of it' (Genesis 28:16).

'The Lord is my light and my salvation – whom shall I fear? ... Though an army besiege me, my heart will not fear ... ' (Psalm 27:1,3).

' ... the darkness will not be dark to you; the night will shine like the day ... ' (Psalm 139:12).

'The light shines in the darkness, the darkness has not overcome it' (John 1:5, RSV).

'In this world you will have trouble. But take heart! I have overcome the world' (John 16:33).

'Jesus came and stood among them and said, "Peace be with you!" ' (John 20:19).

'For I am convinced that neither death nor life, neither angels nor demons, neither the present nor the future, nor any powers, neither height nor depth, nor anything else in all creation, will be able to separate us from the love of God that is in Christ Jesus our Lord' (Romans 8:38–39).

'God is light; in him there is no darkness at all' (1 John 1:5).

PRAYING IN THE DARK NIGHT

At first sight prayer may seem to be simply whistling in the dark, but for Christians in dire straits – those in prison for their faith, for example – it is the clue to triumph and sanity. There are no hard and fast rules, and it is the quality of your presence that matters, not the quantity of time. Short 'arrow' prayers or memorised 'set' prayers can both help us to orient ourselves spiritually. You may want to make up your own prayer poems.

Cries for help

'Lord, save us! We're going to drown!' (Matthew 8:25).

'I do believe; help me overcome my unbelief!' (Mark 9:24).

'Lord Jesus Christ, Son of God, have mercy on me, a sinner' (The Jesus Prayer)

'Come, Lord Jesus' (Revelation 22:20).

Prayers using the psalms

'Lord, lift up the light of your countenance upon us, and we shall be whole' (adapted from the Book of Common Prayer).

'As the deer pants for streams of water, so my soul pants for you, O God' (Psalm 42:1).

'Let me hear joy and gladness; let the bones you have crushed rejoice' (Psalm 51:8).

' . . . my soul thirsts for you, my body longs for you . . .' (Psalm 63:2, BCP).

'Out of the depths I cry to you, O Lord; O Lord, hear my voice . . . My soul waits for the Lord more than watchmen wait for the morning' (Psalm 130:1–2,6).

Prayer poems

Not what thou hast been,
Nor what thou art,
But what thou wouldst be,
Doth God in his mercy consider.   *Anon*

I do not understand
    but I desire truth;
I do not see
    but I desire sight;
I do not know
    but I desire to be known.

Show me yourself, O Lord,
in your glory and your humility,
and in the glory of your humility.
Show me myself, O Lord,
not just as I am,
but as I am in you,
in the humility of your glory.

Lord, it is dark: be my light.   *Philip Seddon*

Glory be to the Father, and to the Son,
and to the Holy Spirit:
As it was in the beginning, is now,
and shall be for ever. Amen.

Some 'do's and 'don'ts

Do have mercy on yourself: God's mercy is higher than your
standards.

Don't reproach yourself that you have taken what you think
is a long time to open up to God: time past is unimportant.
Today is the day of salvation.

Look up Ephesians 4:32.

Do care for yourself: God does.

Don't be so hard on yourself: you're not the Judge.

Look up Matthew 6:25–30.

Do let yourself off the hook: God did not hang you up there.

Do 'lie back and enjoy it' – your favourite music, a meal
with a friend, a night out.

Look up 1 Timothy 6:17 and 1 Corinthians 10:31.

Don't spiritualise: don't disguise a difficult human experience
with unreal or untrue spiritual language. Speak the truth
– or run the risk of laying yourself open to self-deception.

Don't split your life into separate self-contained compartments: your experience of hurt or pain in one area will
affect – or have affected – other parts of you. (That's why
salvation – the process of being made whole – takes time
to work its way through your system!)

Look up Mark 4:1–9.

Don't become obsessed with one particular type or theory of
healing, blessing or promise: God is much more imaginative than we are, and has a unique way of tailoring his
salvation to each person's need.

Do keep yourself in touch with what is going on around you.
Treasure your friends and their wisdom. Ignoring them
and alienating yourself doesn't usually help, and probably
indicates pride on your part

Look up Romans 16.

Do pray for someone to whom you can open your heart in confidence (and maybe regularly).

Do be more concerned to find out what God is wanting to do in you than what he has done in someone else, or what someone else thinks he should do in you.

Look up 1 Samuel 3 and John 5:19.

Do drop the 'should's and 'ought's; instead, adopt the 'can's. The language we use reveals a lot about us. We can choose to live in the prison of obligation ('I ought to be doing far more', 'I shouldn't feel like this') or in the freedom of possibility ('I can do this', 'I can help with . . . ')

Do identify, above all, with Christ. Let Christ be your true role model, the one you follow and are shaped by. Other guides and friends may well reflect him but can never replace him.

Look up Philippians 4:13.

TAKE SEVEN DAYS . . .

> We were made gratuitously and we want to be loved gratuitously.
> We don't want to be loved for our merits.
> > *Gustavo Gutierrez*

Day 1

• Read any of the following Psalms: 22, 41, 42, 43, 63, 88, 130.

When we long for God's presence, we pray. A huge range of emotions (much wider than Christians generally allow!) is expressed in these psalms, for God's people are frequently despised, abused and misunderstood. When we pray with the psalmists, we can admit the problem of the apparent absence and silence of God. There are no short cuts or quick obvious solutions, but expressing our feelings, needs and desires is important. We stop pretending to be very 'spiritual', and accept that we are human, with all the glory and the tragedy which that implies.

Day 2

• Read any of these passages from Job: 3:1–12; 16:6–14; 19:23–27; 38; 39; 40; 41; 42:1–6.

Job is relentless. He passionately yearns to have it out with God: 'What do you think you're up to? Why am I suffering like this?' (St Teresa once said to God in a stormy crossing of a river, 'If this is how you treat your friends, no wonder you have so few!') Job is convinced that God cannot really be his enemy, yet this is what it feels like. God's words to Job out of the storm at the end (chapter 38) are not a complete answer (the New Testament was still to come), but the gist of it is a question to Job: 'If creation is so powerful and complex, how do you think you can ever comprehend the Creator?'

Day 3

• Read John 21:1–4.

Peter, the man of action, decided to go back to his old job. Confused, let down even, his wonderful hopes and expectations dashed, it must have seemed like the sensible thing to do.

• Remember a time when you have felt let down by your Christian faith in some way. Somehow it didn't live up to your expectations or give you what you had thought it promised. Recall what this time of doubt and confusion felt like. How did you cope with this crisis of faith?

The fishermen couldn't even fish successfully any more! Then, with the dawn, Jesus came. At first they didn't recognise him, but when they did, the experience and knowledge of his presence was enough to give them faith to keep following him. How did you come to recognise the presence of Jesus with you in your time of darkness?

• Write about the experience you have just recalled. Pray that you will know that Jesus is with you in any dark situation in your life at present. Allow the light of his presence to give you faith to follow him even though you may see no answers just yet.

Day 4

• Read Mark 14:32–42 and Hebrews 4:14 – 5:10.

We easily forget that Jesus was an absolutely down-to-earth human being. Mark and John again and again emphasise his powerful emotions. No passage does so more than this account of Jesus in Gethsemane, where we see him at the end of his tether – distraught, agonised, overwhelmed with grief and deeply disturbed. This is the cost of human involvement and divine salvation. This is the 'weight of sin' that has to be confronted before the cross is reached, and this is where mighty choices have to be made. Jesus' passion, his willing helplessness and his suffering show that he, too, experienced the deepest of darkness.

Day 5

• Read Philippians 2:5–11.

This early Christian hymn invites us to identify with the Jesus who identified with us. When we are concerned with ascending, we need to see Christ descending all the way, not just in his birth but in his death. This is very much the strange and upside-down path of 'darkness'; if we follow Christ, we follow the one who renounced every claim to power, position, status and 'influence'. Only the person who enters the humility and humiliation of Christ will share his glory.

Day 6

• Read Mark 9:2–10 and 2 Corinthians 3:18.

It is very important not to become obsessed with darkness. The only way of transformation is by light, which continues shining in the darkness that we experience (John 1:5). We are changed and transfigured only by the presence of Christ, which means his birth, baptism, death and resurrection, ascension and giving of the Spirit, and his being in the Trinity. His light is greater than our darkness. We do not need to fear but to see his glory. Of course we often get it wrong, like Peter did (Mark 9:6), but the invitation to 'come and see' is always there.

Day 7

• Read Matthew 11:28–30 and Galatians 5:1.

Burdens, obligations, rules and regulations, expectations of what we ought to be and disappointments with what we are not can take up an awful lot of time and energy, and lead to disillusion and despair. None of this is remotely near the heart of Christ. You can let it all go, along with the past.

What are you hanging on to or afraid of letting go? Real and radical freedom is highly unnerving, even a bit risky! If you want the freedom of the Spirit, you will have to abandon all that holds you captive, so that Christ who abandoned everything can hold you free.

7

IMAGINATION AND SPIRITUALITY

Russ Parker

There is a scene in the film *Nicholas and Alexandra* where the deposed Tsar is standing on the back of the train which is taking him and his family to prison and, ultimately, execution. Tsar Nicholas turns to his guard and asks, 'Was it because I was cruel and a bad ruler that the people hated me?' His guard replies, 'No, it wasn't so much because you were bad. It was because you did not have any imagination. You just did not see the damage you were doing.'

IMAGINATION?
What is 'imagination'? Before we can see how imagination can be a source of spiritual growth, we need to see what it is and does.

• It is the ability to see the significance of things, whether present or absent, and to present this for others to share.

• It is the construction and use of material forms and figures (such as paintings and photographs) to represent real things in another form. Examples are art, or symbolism used in worship.

• It is the ability to locate and develop feelings and images of things which do not exist in the present but which are part of memories, dreams or stories.

Our imaginations give us the capacity to explore reality and to develop our sense of wonder about God and his creation.

Imagination – being truly human

> And God said, 'Let the water teem with living creatures, and let birds fly above the earth across the expanse of the sky.' So God created the great creatures of the sea and every living and moving thing with which the water teems ... And God saw that it was good ... Then God said, 'Let us make man in our image ... '
> *Genesis 1:20–21,26*

It should be no surprise to us that, when we consider God, we see that he created everything imaginatively. He fills the world with a kaleidoscope of colour and life. And at the heart of God's creating is his reflected image: humankind. We, too, are a product of his imagination: we are, indeed, God's imagination enfleshed. Therefore, by nature, people are creative and have freedom to express themselves imaginatively in a riot of gifts and skills. So, approaching life – including our spiritual life – imaginatively is part of what it means to be truly human.

We first begin to use our imagination in our childhood. It is then that we try and enter into the experiences of those around us. Children play games like 'house' and 'war' as a way of identifying with and understanding their parents and the larger events of life. It is a time of story-telling and living through the excitement and adventures of our heroes. Play becomes a creative moment for us to touch and taste the inventions of our minds; it is a vehicle of discovery and learning. Here we learn to include others in our world of make-believe. Our imagination provides some of the building blocks for sharing and communicating our ideas. This gives us a sense of self-identity, of who we are, and of belonging to a particular community.

We can take a new step forward in our spiritual lives as we discover again some of the imaginative processes that we knew as children – not to imagine make-believe, but to reach out for a spiritual maturity which could be, but which, for us, is 'not yet'. Using our imagination wisely can increase our awareness of who we are as Christians, of what it means to belong to the church and of what God is doing among us.

A vision shared
One of the main ways that we share imagination is through art, whether it is in the form of painting, sculpture, drama or music. All art is a vehicle of expression for the imagination. It is an attempt to represent reality or to convey something of the meaning which the artist sees in the world around him. It is essentially an act of sharing. We are being invited to examine the work and to appreciate imaginatively the significance of the original as perceived by the painter or writer or composer. The message of each work of art may be to create something of beauty or to present a challenge or critical comment. Therefore a painting of a pastoral scene or a photograph of a war-torn people are both art because they are representations of reality as understood by the artist. They convey a message which the artist has heard and which he wishes to convey imaginatively in another form to us.

Sharing symbols
The sharing of imagination can also be seen in our use and appreciation of symbols. Some symbols are used so widely that they are universally recognised. Symbols common in the West include the wearing of a wedding ring and the bride wearing white, or having a black arm-band as a token of respect for someone who has died. For the Christian, the cross is a symbol of Christ's death and resurrection for the forgiveness of our sins. So, when we focus on the cross, we don't stop at the superficial level of the symbol; our imagination enables us to enter into the meaning and power of the work of God which it represents. So symbols are effective, not because they are ends in themselves (as though they were magic talismans), but because they sum up, or represent, a greater reality.

Some symbols are not static but dynamic in that they are a kind of drama involving others. An example of this is the laying on of hands or anointing with oil for healing. Here the recipient has actual contact with his symbols and is helped to concentrate on the healing presence of Jesus Christ. So symbols are to be triggers which 'kick us into life' imaginatively and so enable us to make connection with the spiritual reality of what God has done and is doing. An imaginative response is part of each step of faith.

Danger!

Responding imaginatively to spiritual things is a necessary, but risky, part of growth. Symbols divorced from imagination lead to superstition. If this happens, the symbol or act becomes its own message or has its own power. Thus imagination has been disengaged and the symbol becomes a fixed image with little room left for the imagination to work.

Because we are sinful and fallen creatures, our imagination has made nightmares of our world. In Genesis 6:5 we are told that, after the fall of Adam, God declared that the imagination of man's heart was continually evil. This led to a very strong tradition within Jewish teaching that there was a divine law warranting the renunciation of the imaginative impulse. However, through the saving and restoring work of Jesus Christ, we are being reclaimed and renewed. So the Christian gospel is in no way under threat from the imagination. As the Spirit of God works in our lives, he is waiting to release our imagination in order that we use it to grow in faith and develop a richer spirituality.

INVITATION TO IMAGINING

'Now glory be to God who by his mighty power at work within us is able to do far more than we would ever dare to ask or even dream of – infinitely beyond our highest prayers, desires, thoughts or hopes' (Ephesians 3:20, The Living Bible). What an invitation this is from God to dare to imagine what blessings he has in store for us! Yet it seems that not even our wildest dreams can fully grasp what God himself imagines for us. Instead of using our creative gifts for self-centred ends, we are to apply our imaginative faculties in discovering the purposes of God and then to share our insights with a waiting world. This is not a development of new doctrines; it is a sharpening of our spiritual awareness and a means by which we enter more fully into the gospel truths we already know. But before we look at how we can respond imaginatively to God, it is important to see examples of how God has communicated imaginatively with us.

Prophetic imagination

The prophets provide many examples. Isaiah, by walking naked through the streets of Jerusalem, riveted the imagination of the wayward nation on the horrors of exile. It was a compelling and prophetic challenge for them to turn from their disastrous policies and be properly obedient to Yahweh. Jeremiah meditated upon the potter at his wheel and gained insights into how God could remould an intransigent people. Ezekiel played siege games with an imaginary Jerusalem using the shavings from his own hair and so spoke powerfully to his audience about the consequences of disobedience. Agabus, as we read in Acts, did not merely tell Paul of the captivity that lay ahead for him; he wrapped himself in the apostle's leather belt and let the imagery speak for itself.

These examples show how prophetic impact was heightened by the use of symbols which appealed to the imagination and allowed people to reflect upon the divine word contained within them. It is important to note that the use of symbols was not to be divorced from the facts: there was the accompanying prophetic word of truth. This combination of word and symbol is seen clearly in the ministry of Jesus.

Jesus – imagination in ministry

Almost the whole of Jesus' ministry is an appeal to the imagination. His teaching employed a wealth of imagery and story. When speaking about his work, he pictured himself as 'the gate', 'the good shepherd' and 'the true vine'. Rather than give doctrinal definitions of salvation, he told parables. It was for people such as Paul and the Gospel writers to reflect upon these stories and pictures and formulate doctrines and beliefs. Jesus gave no lecture on heaven; instead he filled the imagination of his disciples with pictures of the 'pearl of great price' or of a fisherman dragging in a net at the end of a working day. There were ideas of a 'great house' with room for the faithful or a 'banquet' for those of all classes who simply had time for the Master's words. (This is not to say that he did not also teach systematically, as the Sermon on the Mount illustrates.)

Jesus appealed to the childlike qualities within his disciples, essential if they were to make progress on their spiritual journey: 'I tell you the truth, unless you change and become like little children, you will never enter the kingdom of heaven' (Matthew 18:3). Jesus challenged his followers to recapture something of the childlike sense of wonder and openness, to keep their imaginations alive! How many of Jesus' hearers would have laughed at the idea of a plank of wood sticking out of someone's eye (Matthew 7:3) or felt saddened at the predicament of the Lost Son (Luke 15:11–32). By using pictures and stories, Jesus enabled his hearers to use their imaginations to identify with the issues at stake and to enter into them more fully by engaging their feelings and thoughts. Imagination offers us a chance to do what Jesus' hearers did: to appreciate with both 'head' and 'heart' matters of spiritual significance. Let us now look at some of the ways the imagination can be employed on our spiritual journey.

IMAGINATION AT WORK

Icons
The use of visual imagery has long been common in Christian circles. Perhaps one of the most exquisite forms has been that of icons, an art form developed by the Eastern Church. Each painting was to be a work of faith and prayer and was closely examined to ensure that it was doctrinally acceptable. The individual character of the artist (or group of artist monks) was not to show in the work, in order to underline the primacy of divine authority. The overall aim was to prevent interferences from the human personality out of deference to the infinite nature of the Divine Creator himself. Standardised gold-leaf backgrounds and stylised two-dimensional features

were used in order to focus the attention of the faithful on the sacred mystery represented rather than on the representation itself. So an icon is not a work of art which points to the artist, but a work which points to God.

Part of the way in which such icons 'work' is by using symbolism. We may need the key to unlock the meaning hidden in the symbols; we need to 'learn the language' which the artist is speaking. For example, in the Mother of God odigitria icon, Mary is pointing to her child: a symbol that Jesus is 'the way, the truth and the life'. Jesus holds the scroll of the Law in his left hand and gives a sign of blessing with his right: symbols that he is both the just Judge and merciful Saviour. Similarly, the letters within Jesus' halo (which mean, 'He who is') proclaim his divinity. Coupled with his portrayal as human, we have a powerful symbol of Jesus as fully human and fully divine.

Icons demand a particular way of looking. We are not to worship the image but to worship the God to whom the image points. Therefore, an icon is not so much to be looked at as looked through. This may explain the common practice of portraying the eyes of Christ as expressionless: the onlooker is invited to travel through the vacant regard of the image towards our transcendent God rather than linger at the purely human level of expression.

Looking through an icon is the first step in worship. For example, if the picture was of Mary and Jesus, then the worshipper was to look through the eyes of the mother and enter into her feelings of wonder and privilege at being the mother of the Christ. The whole reality of her special grace and station would be perceived and the individual would for a moment touch upon the mystery of the incarnation. This would bring him to a deeper and fuller worship of God himself for his great grace. If the focus was upon Jesus, then by a similar approach the worshipper would enter into the whole subject of God's wondrous gift of his Son for sinners. So the icon was to be used as an initial stepping stone for the imagination to meditate upon the reality of the mystery of God. This was not to be a merely cerebral exercise but an engaging of the whole person: feelings, mind and spirit.

Dreams and spiritual growth

A cursory glance at the Bible will readily reveal that God used dreams to communicate with people. Joseph, Mary and the infant Jesus were saved from the murderous hands of Herod by a dream in which a message was spoken directly. The Egyptians were able to prepare for seven years of famine through the interpretation of some dreams which contained a good deal of symbolism. The Bible stories do not seem to indicate that God speaks only through particular kinds of dream. The implication of this is that God can use our dreams to communicate with us. Interestingly enough, the Hebrew term for dreaming means 'to make whole or healthy', and so we can equally conclude that dreaming is good for us.

Basically our dreams are our own creations. It is as if our imaginations write a number of 'scripts' each night based largely upon our current experiences. We can also have nightmares or recurring dreams which disturb us, and this underlines that dreaming may reflect some 'unfinished business' in our lives. Our dreams to a large degree mirror how we are truly feeling and sometimes reflect things which we may be unaware of in waking life. Therefore, in recalling our dreams we need to pay special attention to our feelings. The symbols and pictures of the dream, which are the product of the imagination, may symbolise or represent things which we can identify. By clarifying the feelings we have and connecting them with the symbols, and, where appropriate, acting upon the dream, we will gain a more complete appreciation of ourselves and so have occasion to offer this to God for his touch of blessing.

For example, I counselled a woman who kept dreaming of a little girl in a soiled dress being kept forcibly on a man's lap. The prayer approach I used with this dream was to ask the question which God addressed to Adam, 'Where are you?' (Genesis 3:9). What followed in this particular instance was a meditation on the dream picture, picking up the woman's feelings which were mainly concerned with helplessness, feeling dirty and guilty. These were then offered to Christ for healing and forgiveness. As we followed this process, there came a moment of clarity when the woman was able to share that she had been repressing for years feelings of guilt because she had been sexually abused by a member of her family. She had not been able to tell anyone for fear of exposure and rejection. It became clear that the little girl of the dream was herself and so the final stage in the meditation approach to the dream was to offer the little girl the forgiveness and love of Jesus. Her imagination helped her to see Jesus entering the room and freeing the girl and even giving her a clean white dress to wear. The effect of this work with her dream was to release her from a lifetime of guilt and insecurity and to renew her marriage.

Faith imagination

All of us have memories of our experiences of life. No matter how old they may be, there are times in our lives when something triggers them and we relive their times and feelings again. These may be pleasant and we enjoy remembering good days, or they may be painful and we wish we could be free of their power and hold upon our lives. The ministry of inner healing, or healing the memories, attempts to deal with the latter kind of memories and bring the healing power of Jesus into the area of crippling negative thoughts. Inner healing is a process of emotional reconstruction under the guidance of the Holy Spirit whereby, through Christ, people can have power over their memories and manage their lives with greater freedom. At the heart of this ministry is the use of visualisation or faith-imagination.

> Visualising and/or verbalising is putting your faith into action. It gets God's promises from our heads into our hearts. This is what I see happening in inner-healing prayer.   *Rita Bennett*

An example of how this might work could be seen in the person who finds him/herself unable to cope with his/her emotions and who may be suffering from depression, fear or anxiety. The start would be a faith-focusing upon the person of the Lord Jesus Christ. This means that the person would be encouraged to see or sense the presence of the Lord Jesus and to allow the biblical truth of such statements as 'I will never leave you nor forsake you' (Joshua 1:5) or 'And surely I am with you always, to the very end of the age' (Matthew 28:20) to become a picture in which they see Jesus demonstrating this truth for them. The next step would be an invitation to Jesus to come into the hurting feelings and, where possible, to bring to mind and heart an actual memory which directly relates to the hurt in question.

All the while the person is focusing his faith upon Jesus and getting in touch with the memory unfolding inside, he will be verbalising his imagination and feelings with the one praying with him. After the memory has been clarified, any hurting feelings are identified and offered to the Lord for healing. This is to act directly on the scripture which says, 'For we have not an high priest which cannot be touched with the feeling of our infirmities . . . ' (Hebrews 4:15, AV). So we actually invite and visualise Jesus touching our hurts and painful moments. There may also be a need to include a prayer of forgiveness for any person who has caused these hurts. What this does is to allow the acceptance and love of Jesus to overcome feelings of anger, shame or bitterness about the past. Forgiveness releases the person being counselled to gain some perspective on his past and to move away from its destructive power to get on with his life.

The final step in the inner-healing process is to offer thanksgiving to God for any new insights and healing gained. Celebration always followed healing in the stories the Bible records. Joseph threw his arms around Benjamin and wept as he shared how God had given him a new perspective on his years of slavery. The father of the Lost Son remembered better times and welcomed his son home. The two disciples on the road to Emmaus went dashing back to the disciples in Jerusalem when Jesus healed their thinking about what happened at Calvary. Naturally, the new outlook which prayer has brought needs to be worked out and applied by choice and faith. There may be challenges, but the love of Jesus has brought release and we need to apply our faith to the new ground gained. Then we are able to love our neighbour more completely and be a channel of Christ's love to one another. Inner healing is a ministry like any other, to help us to grow up and be mature in our faith and sharing.

God can restore the mind to life; we can't, any more than we can create new brain tissue; but where there is that sense of life which the love of Jesus Christ brings, we can give ourselves to the task of replacing destructive feelings in old, sick memories with new rich images of the love of God. These new images lead to whole, constructive living.

> O memory of a painful time,
> Are you seed or stone?
> A dark and deadly tomb,
> Or seed with life to bloom?
> Only if I say, 'I want you',
> Will I really know.
>
> O sprouting seed, are you angry
> At the dark and choking dirt?
> What grates your tender shoot
> And blocks your chosen route?
> Only if I say, 'I forgive you',
> Will I really know.
>
> Author unknown (from *Healing Harvest*)

A thousand-and-one ways
One of the delights about responding imaginatively to God is that there is always the possibility of something new: we can never finally catalogue all the ways in which our imaginations can take us deeper into God. We have looked in detail at three: icons, dreams and the healing of memories. Some are so commonly used that we hardly think of our response as 'imaginative' – such as the symbol of the cross. Some imaginative responses to God are followed up elsewhere in this book, particularly in the chapter on meditating on scripture and the chapters on prayer; but be open to the possibility of God doing something new in you. The exercises which follow will give you a taster of what is possible.

> 'No eye has seen,
>   no ear has heard,
> no mind has conceived

what God has prepared for
those who love him.'   *1 Corinthians 2:9*

TAKE SEVEN DAYS ...

Before beginning any of the exercises, it is important that
you are aware that they may not all be suitable for you.
This may be either because the particular way of using the
imagination is difficult for you, or because you do not feel
comfortable getting in touch with your subjective feelings. If
either is the case, then don't be unduly alarmed; just accept
that this kind of approach is not for you. Try to make a point
of sharing your work with a trusted friend who can help you
check out and clarify what you have been doing.

Imaginative contemplation of the Gospels is a very ancient
tradition in the Church.

> Hear and see these things being narrated, as though
> you were hearing with your own ears and seeing with
> your own eyes, for these things are most sweet to him
> who thinks of them with desire, and even more so to
> him who tastes them. And although many of these
> things are narrated as past events, you must meditate
> on them all as though they were happening in the
> present moments because in this way you will certainly
> taste a greater sweetness ... Bring before your eyes
> past actions as though they were present. Then you
> will feel how full of wisdom and delight they are.
>
> *Rudolph of Saxony*, 14th century
> (from the preface to *Vita Christi*)

Day 1 Bringing your gift to Jesus

This first exercise is a meditation based on Peter's encounter
with Jesus on the shore of the Sea of Galilee. It offers some
suggestions as to what the encounter meant for Peter and, by
inviting you to experience the scene, it also invites you to
meditate on your own relationship with Jesus.

• First, spend a minute or so just relaxing. Make sure that

you are in a comfortable position either sitting or lying down. Allow yourself to become aware of whatever background noises there are and, having done this, put them aside so that you can concentrate upon this exercise.

• Now read John 21:1–19.

• Imagine yourself alongside Peter in the boat. Like him you may have been working hard through the day and you might have a number of things on your mind about your walk with Jesus. You can see the shore which is not too far off and there, standing on the beach, is Jesus. How does it feel to be in the boat knowing that Jesus is standing on the shore ready to meet with you?

• Once you have become aware of Jesus waiting for you, it is time to leave the boat and get close to him. See yourself leaping into the water and wading through the waves to get to the shore. How does this feel, to be pushing through the water to meet with the Lord?

• As you reach the shore, Jesus is standing there, waiting for you. Look at him and allow yourself to get in touch with the full importance of this moment . . . 'Jesus is waiting for me'. How does he greet you?

• After a while you realise that you have a personal gift to offer to him. It can be anything you choose. So, when you are ready, give Jesus your gift. How does he receive it? What does he do with your gift?

• Allow yourself to become fully aware of any feelings you have as you see Jesus receiving your gift.

• Soon it will be time to leave this shore but, before you leave, Jesus has a gift to give you. It may be some words, a touch, a picture or something that he has made for you. For Peter it was some words of challenge. Give yourself time to see what it is that Jesus offers you and take it from him. Show your thanks in any way you wish. How does it feel to have this gift from Jesus? What will you do with it?

• It is time to say your final words to him. He is there for you and wants to send you on your way with his blessing. With your gift from Jesus, see yourself moving on in your life to the next stage in your journey.

• Now bring this exercise to a close. Become aware of the room you are in and close with a prayer of thanks to the Lord. You might like to make some notes which will help you in your future journey with the Lord.

(For further examples of this use of the Bible see *Imagining the Gospels*, Kathy Galloway, SPCK 1988.)

Day 2 Knowing God as Father

> . . . underneath are the everlasting arms.
>
> *Deuteronomy 33:27*

• If possible, find a picture or photograph of a new-born child resting in the arms of its loving father. Use your imagination to try and become this child, so new and vulnerable yet resting in the arms of his/her Father.

As a help to this, read the words of the poem below and, for now, let them be yours, offered to our heavenly Father.

> I am just born!
> Me you are healing, restoring.
> Building within me a cathedral for your spirit.
> Out of the dark I came,
> from the captive stronghold of fear;
> birthed by the power of Jesus,
> into the hands of the Father.
>
> I am just born!
> Chosen before all eternity.
> Weightless in your arms I lie,
> surrounded by love.
> Expectant I wait,
> held in your gaze of love,
> for you will restore to me the lost years.

Yours before ever earthly parents claimed me;
I am your child:
Me you are holding.
The kingdom of heaven is breaking upon me.
I am just born!   *S Larkin*

Look once again at the picture and imagine how it feels to
be vulnerable and yet cared for. Let your imagination take
you deeper into what it means to be God's new-born child.
Enjoy his protection and care. Rejoice that your heavenly
Father has got your world in his hands. Give thanks for your
new life from God.

• You may wish to write down some of the things which
especially help or challenge you about being a child of God
in need of his protection and care.

Day 3 Healing prayer and the ring of peace
This meditation should enable us to go deeper in praying for
the healing of our friends.

• Begin by recollecting the presence of Christ. If you are
praying in a group, then remind yourself of the promise of
Jesus, 'For where two or three come together in my name,
there am I with them' (Matthew 18:20).

• So there you are, you and Jesus. What sort of experience
is it to be in his presence? He 'is the same yesterday and
today and for ever' (Hebrews 13:8). He is the same healer
and shepherd as ever. He is the same Jesus who gave this
promise: 'Peace I leave with you; my peace I give you' (John
14:27). So open yourself to Jesus and let his peace fill you
and surround you.

• There is no need to strive for peace: 'let the peace of
Christ rule in your hearts' (Colossians 3:15). See yourself
surrounded by the 'ring of God's peace'. You might visualise
this as the ring of chariots of fire which surrounded Elisha
(2 Kings 6:16–18). The peace of God is one with the power
of God, and the love and joy of God. To be within God's

'ring of peace' is to be in the place of creativity, security and healing.

• So be still and let God's peace flow into every part of you; your body, mind and spirit. Make this an opportunity to rest in the Lord Jesus.

• When the time is right, bring others – perhaps your family and home, or church fellowship – into the ring of peace. Thank God that he wants the places you have thought of to be places of peace. Imagine that peace reaching out from Jesus, through you, to them. Bring also into this ring any that you know who are ill or are in trouble. Visualise each one as a person created and loved by God and imagine how their lives will benefit from the peace of God. See them in your ring of peace being open to the will of God for their lives. Then give thanks to God for them and for his healing will for their lives and pray that his 'will be done [for them] on earth as it is in heaven'. This exercise helps us to pray simply for God's will to be done and to offer ourselves as channels for his will.

(This meditation is adapted from *Invitation to Healing*, by Roy Lawrence, Kingsway 1979.)

Day 4 Practising the presence of Christ

For in him we live and move and have our being.
Acts 17:28

• As you go through the next twenty-four hours, take a few moments to stop and focus on the presence of Jesus there with you. You may be at work or in your home, walking or sitting down. In your imagination, 'turn your eyes upon Jesus, look full in his wonderful face'. Give yourself some space to feel the impact of Christ with you and note any changed perspective this might give you. Then in a simple prayer, ask God to give you grace to walk in this new light you have received. Jesus may give you some insights about your behaviour or about people around you. Make a note of these when you can and use them as a basis for prayer.

Repeat the exercise as you go through your day. At the end of the day, reflect on what you have learnt about yourself or things around you and give thanks to God. It may help to make a diary or journal of these insights and so give you a record to show how you have grown spiritually.

> He comes
>
> Christ comes
> again and again He comes
> walking into our today,
> challenging us, leading us, loving us
> into responding anew to His call . . .
>
> He comes
> that we might live,
> to dream with daring,
> and pray with hope
> for a potency that creates
> into reality,
> a decent life for all.   *Karol*

Day 5 Group exercise on forgiveness
This exercise is suitable for a group ranging from six to a dozen people.

• Sit in a circle and have one member read out John 20: 21–23. Then give some time to focus upon the presence of Jesus in the group.

• Now invite people to sit with both hands open and touching the hands of people on either side. In a period of silent confession allow all the sins which are to be confessed to be 'felt' in the palm of the left hand.

• At a suitable moment ask everyone literally to place the sins to be confessed into the open right hand of the person sitting on your left. As you receive these confessions close your right hand over them.

• Then, in obedience to the words of Jesus to be channels of forgiveness to each other, raise your right hand into the air and open it, letting these sins go into the hands of the Lord Jesus. In so doing we are declaring that through the ministry of the priesthood of all believers, Jesus is releasing us from our sins and pouring out his forgiveness.

• With your now empty left hand imagine the forgiveness of Jesus being given to you as a gift, and so close this hand when you receive your forgiveness from him.

Day 6 Faith imagination prayer
This is a prayer form which can be used in circumstances where there is some blockage preventing personal growth, your own or some else's.

• Read Matthew 17:20–21 and in your mind's eye focus upon the person or situation you wish to see changed. What are the main issues which need healing or help?

• Now see Jesus walking into these moments and notice any changes that start to take place. Pick up any significant words spoken by Jesus or actions he performs. Perhaps people begin to take on different roles or develop new attitudes. Maybe the situations begin to look different.

• It is these differences which you see Jesus making that you can now take hold of in faith and begin to thank God for.

Day 7 Dream work
The following are some ground rules for recording and working with your own dreams. While not every dream will deal with matters of major importance, working with dreams will give you more awareness of yourself and what you think and feel. And remember, Jesus wishes to become Lord of every new awareness we gain.

• Before going to sleep, pray that God will help you to remember any significant dreams. Commit your sleep to him.

> In the last days, God says,
> I will pour out my Spirit on all people.

130

> Your sons and daughters will prophesy,
> your young men will see visions,
> your old men will dream dreams.   *Acts 2:17*

• Keep a pen and paper beside your bed and make sure you have easy access to a light. When you wake, immediately write down as much of the dream detail as possible. Add as many associations to your dream as you can, including links into recent events which seem to fit the dream story.

• Write down any feelings either contained in the dream or which arise as a result from the dream. It is these which will offer clues to what the dream is really saying. What does the dream appear to be saying at first glance?

• Now bring the dream picture and its message to the Lord and see, in your imagination, how Jesus responds. As you do this, include in your prayers any truths, challenges or convictions which have been on your heart. This may give an opportunity to see a possible next step in your journey with Christ.

• If you have difficulty in understanding your dream, it may help to imagine each part or symbol of the dream as having 'a voice of its own'; for example, if you dream of a tall dark stranger, then become that stranger and see if you can get 'inside' the character and speak what seems to be appropriate. This may help to clarify the dream.

THE HEALING SQUARE

• Take a blank sheet of paper and draw a large square on it.

• Slowly and prayerfully look back on your life at the times you were hurt.

• Write within the square the names (initials) of any people who have hurt you. Think of whom you fear, avoid or judge harshly.

• Put a circle around those who are not close to you now. Pick one of these and tell Jesus how you feel. Be as honest and objective as you can.

• When you can see why that person may have hurt you, put a vertical line through their name.

• When you feel that you can say to them what Christ would say, then draw a horizontal line through their name. By the cross they are forgiven.

• If you can see that you were part of the problem, and can forgive yourself, then put an 'X' through that name.

• Now ask God to help you draw whatever good from that time of hurt he allows. Give him thanks for his healing and your growth.

• Now ask God to show you ways that will be appropriate for you to build a drawbridge between you and this person.

• Once you have completed work on this memory and are ready to continue, repeat the exercise as the Lord leads you.

8

PHYSICAL SPIRITUALITY

Amiel Osmaston

'Physical spirituality! What do you mean?' may have been your reaction to the title of this chapter. Many people think that the body and the spirit are two separate entities, generally in conflict with each other, and that to become truly spiritual one must try to be as un-physical as possible. This chapter is an exploration of a more positive, creative and fully Christian understanding of the vital role that our bodies play in our spirituality.

> That God, all Spirit, served with Spirits, associated to Spirits, should have such an affection, such a love to this body, this earthly body, this deserves wonder. The Father was pleased to breathe into this body, at first, in the Creation; the Son was pleased to assume this body himself, after, in the Redemption; the Holy Ghost is pleased to consecrate this body, and make it his Temple, by his sanctification ...
>
> *John Donne*

God has made us physical beings. Our bodies are involved in all our communicating, with each other and with God himself. We express our worship, our prayers and our response to God as physical beings: we listen to him and learn from him; we serve and obey him. Some of the ways in which we do this have become so traditional and stylised that we hardly think of them as 'using our bodies' at all. For instance, do you kneel to pray? If so, you are using your body in a particular way which helps you to concentrate on praying, and which expresses your humility before the Lord Almighty.

Your body is involved in everything spiritual that you do, whether you want it to be or not and whether you are aware of it or not. All human spirituality is to some extent physical. This can be a source of tremendous richness and vitality in your spiritual life. The problem is that, if you ignore the role which your body plays, then your spiritual life is likely to be impoverished or even hindered. For instance, if you are not by nature a 'night owl', yet you regularly have your time of prayer last thing at night when your body is tired, tense or sleepy, then it will not be surprising if you find prayer unsatisfying, hard going, and have difficulties in concentrating.

We need to become more aware of the ways in which the aspects of ourselves which we generally label as 'physical' or 'spiritual' are actually inseparable and influence each other. Then we can reduce the negative influences and explore the positive ones more deeply.

BODY AND SPIRIT AFFECT EACH OTHER

The body certainly affects the spirit. What you do physically has a strong influence on your spiritual state. We are to be like dedicated soldiers, or athletes in training (2 Timothy 2:3–5). A Christian's lifestyle should not be one of over-indulgence, with excesses of over-eating, drinking, smoking or abuse of drugs or illicit sex. Likewise we should not neglect or abuse our bodies unnecessarily by lack of exercise, bad eating habits, stress and overwork. All these are likely to undermine and damage one's spiritual life. On the positive side, it has long been recognised that discipline of the body through fasting can be of great spiritual benefit.

> Do you not know that your body is a temple of the Holy Spirit, who is in you, whom you have received from God? You are not your own; you were bought at a price. Therefore honour God with your body.
>
> *1 Corinthians 6:19–20*

A physical lifestyle that does not honour or glorify God will have destructive results for spiritual growth.

Just as the body affects the spirit, so it is equally true that the spirit affects the body. You can often discern things about a person's spiritual state by seeing the effect it is having on their body. An extreme example of this is demonic possession, when satanic forces can actually take over control of a person's movements and speech. Paul writes about the powerful influence of spiritual sin on the physical body in the context of sharing the Lord's Supper.

> For anyone who eats and drinks without recognising the body of the Lord eats and drinks judgment on himself. That is why many among you are weak and sick, and a number of you have fallen asleep.
>
> *1 Corinthians 11:29–30*

Of course, the spirit can affect the body in positive ways too. Recently many churches in Britain and in other countries have experienced a wave of spiritual renewal. Large numbers of Christians have found themselves (often to their own surprise!) responding to the inner working of the Holy Spirit with outward physical manifestations such as laughter, tears, trembling, falling to the ground and 'resting in the Spirit' for an hour or more. Naturally we cannot assume that these physical responses are all caused purely by the Holy Spirit; in some cases the causes may be at least partly psychological. However, for many people the experience of 'letting go' spiritually and physically, and opening up afresh to God, certainly seems to have grown in them the 'fruit of the Spirit', and they have discovered that their love for Christ has deepened and their confidence in witnessing increased.

I have talked and prayed with several people who have been harbouring resentment or hatred for years and have finally been able to bring themselves to forgive the person who wronged them. They have found that the spiritual release has also released them from physical symptoms such as migraines, twitches, high blood pressure, arthritis or paralysis. (Of course the root cause of these illnesses is not always a spiritual one.)

As a final example of the way the spirit affects the body, I remember a small child who pointed at an elderly, humble and deeply prayerful member of our church, and whispered to me, 'I bet she's a Christian, 'cos she looks all sort of nice and shiny!'

THE ROOTS OF OUR ATTITUDES

The Hebrew view of human beings, which we find in the Old Testament, is that each of us is a complex unity. God has created each person as body, as mind and as spirit, with a will and emotions. Each aspect is vital and is a precious gift from God which we must not neglect or despise. Wholeness, health and blessedness (expressed in the Hebrew word *Shalom*) are seen in the person who combines physical action, wisdom and holiness. Our bodily, mental and spiritual characteristics all play a role as the Holy Spirit works to shape each of us into a harmonious whole.

This was the view of Jesus, and his followers too. However, early Christian thinkers and writers were increasingly influenced by the Greek philosophy of the times and especially by Plato. Platonic philosophy was dualistic, believing that bodies and spirits were two separate entities. The spirit was seen as caged temporarily within the decaying matter of a physical body. (This may seem like a purely academic issue, but in fact it deeply affected peoples' beliefs and actions.) Gradually this very negative attitude to the body infiltrated Christianity and led to two opposite distortions. Some people whipped and punished their own bodies in order to subdue and weaken the imprisoning cage and set the spirit free. Others concluded that the spirit was so infinitely superior to physical matter that it could not be affected by it; you could indulge in whatever physical excesses you wished without causing any harm to your spiritual state. These distortions stand as a warning of the dangerous results of a false understanding of the physical body.

It is important to recognise how much our attitudes to the body have been shaped by platonic philosophy and that they are actually quite unbiblical. To see this clearly we must

look carefully at what the Bible has to say about our physical
bodies and how they are involved in our spirituality.

BODIES – A BIBLICAL VIEW

'The body' at the heart of our faith
It is amazing that the central beliefs of the Christian faith and
God's greatest acts in creation and redemption all focus in
some way on human bodies.

• In creation, God made humankind in his own image, out
of the dust of the earth, and he saw that it was good.

• In the incarnation, God in Christ became flesh, growing
in Mary's womb and entering fully into our physical
humanity. He was not a divine Spirit temporarily inhabiting
the disguise of a convenient but degrading physical body. He
actually became human. He experienced the delights, frus-
trations and hurts of being physical.

• In his crucifixion, Christ's body was battered and wounded
for us. Therefore the central act of worship for Christians
down the centuries and across the world has focused on
sharing that body and blood. It is a physical memorial of a
physical event which had world-shattering spiritual implications.

• In the resurrection, Christ was raised from death – body
and all. The tomb was empty. So also for those who follow
Christ; 'we believe in the resurrection of the body'. This
earthly body will be transformed into a heavenly body. But
it will still be a body, and its purpose will still be the same:
an essential part of what makes 'me'. And as 'me' – body
and all – I will be able to rejoice, and to enjoy and glorify
God.

A look at the Old Testament
In the Old Testament there is a healthy and positive attitude
towards the physical body, full of awe and delight at God's
gift.

137

> For you created my inmost being;
>> you knit me together in my mother's womb.
> I praise you because I am fearfully and wonderfully
>> made ...   *Psalm 139:13–14*

The Song of Songs is full of frank and simple enjoyment of the beloved's physical beauty and of pleasure in the use of the senses.

God's people are frequently encouraged to use their bodies to express themselves to God in prayer and worship. Here are a few of the many examples.

• Singing: 1 Chronicles 16:23, Isaiah 12:5, Psalms 30:4; 66:2; 100:2.

• Making Music: 2 Chronicles 7:6, Psalms 98:4–6; 150:3–6.

• Clapping: Psalm 47:1.

• Leaping and Dancing: Psalms 149:3; 150:4. Israelite worship certainly seems to have been energetic. There are at least eight different Hebrew words used to describe various forms of skipping, leaping, whirling and dancing. Miriam the prophetess led the women in a dance of praise to God after the crossing of the Red Sea (Exodus 15:20–21). King David danced at the head of a procession entering Jerusalem.

> David, wearing a linen ephod, danced before the Lord with all his might, while he and the entire house of Israel brought up the ark of the Lord with shouts and the sound of trumpets.   *2 Samuel 6:14–15*

• Prostration: When confronted by a vision of God's power and glory, the response of the prophets was often to fall flat on their faces as an expression of humility and awe (eg Ezekiel 1:28). Other physical gestures of respect included kneeling, shielding the eyes from God's glory or taking off one's shoes on holy ground.

By comparison with all this, most modern Western habits of worship – both corporate and private – seem very rigid, inhibited and inexpressive!

The physical and spiritual are not only closely linked in expressing worship, but also in the ways God chooses to communicate with his people. God often reveals a spiritual message through physical actions and dramatic symbolism. For instance, Ezekiel was commanded to foreshadow the siege and destruction of Jerusalem by lying bound in front of a clay model of the city for 430 days (Ezekiel 4 and 5). Jeremiah had to spoil a linen belt to show the coming ruin of Judah (Jeremiah 13:1–11). Hosea was instructed to marry an adulteress in order to provide a physical demonstration of God's love for unfaithful Israel (Hosea 1, 2 and 3).

A look at the New Testament

The positive Jewish understanding of the body's place in spirituality was carried on into the early Christian church. Paul expressed it clearly.

> I urge you, brothers, in view of God's mercy, to offer your bodies as living sacrifices, holy and pleasing to God – this is your spiritual act of worship.
>
> *Romans 12:1*

The whole person – body and spirit – must be involved in the offering of worship. The physical offering is spiritual worship.

The early Christians followed a Messiah who had come not just to preach a spiritual gospel but to show his Father's love and power by making the blind see, the deaf hear and the lame leap for joy (Matthew 11:2–6, Luke 4:18–21). Jesus cared for and ministered to both body and spirit. He was not a body-denying ascetic.

Unfortunately, centuries of confusion have existed in the Christian Church caused by the contrast of the Greek word *sarx* (literally 'flesh') with 'the spirit' (eg Romans 7:18 – 8:14). Until recently, all English translations of the Bible set 'flesh' in conflict with 'spirit':

> For I know that nothing good dwells within me, that is, in my flesh ... To set the mind on the flesh is

death, but to set the mind on the Spirit is life and
peace.   *Romans 7:18 and 8:6, RSV*

However, by *sarx* Paul did not mean 'the physical body': a
more accurate meaning is given by the New International
Version translation – 'the sinful nature'. What conflicts with
the spirit is not the body, but our sinful, selfish, disobedient
human nature which repeatedly turns its back on God.

If this seems to be an over-emphasis of the physical aspects
of our spirituality, it is because Christians have inherited an
unbalanced view which needs correction. We must ensure
that our attitudes are truly biblical and not distorted by false
philosophies or misunderstandings. With our bodies and with
all that we are and have and do, we must seek to glorify
God.

USING YOUR BODY IN PRAYER AND WORSHIP

With a biblical foundation, we can go on to explore a whole
range of ideas and suggestions as to how you can put all this
into practice. Most of it is intended for use on your own, but
many of the comments and exercises would be equally relevant and suitable for small Bible study and prayer groups,
and a few could even be tried in church services.

'Be still, and know that I am God'

'Using your body in worship' does not necessarily mean leaping around. In fact one of the most important ways in which
your body is involved in your prayer life is in learning to be
deeply still. The body needs to be wholly relaxed and yet
thoroughly alert so that you can concentrate on God without
feeling distracted, uncomfortable, tense, fidgety or sleepy. It
is possible to be both relaxed and alert, but it takes practice.

> Half an hour's listening is essential except when you
> are very busy. Then a full hour is needed.
> *St Francis de Sales*

• Alertness. What wakes you up? Tea? A shower? Fresh air?
Whatever it is, try to do it before you pray. Then do some

140

gentle stretching exercises to get the blood circulating. Concentrate on stretching the part of the body where you generally store your tension. People vary in this. Do you tend to get stiff shoulders, jaw, hands, thighs, stomach or neck?

• Relaxation. In order to get rid of distracting muscle tensions before your pray, lie on the floor on your back. Concentrate on each limb and part of your body in turn, tensing it hard for a few seconds (while keeping the rest of your body relaxed) and then releasing it. As you do so, offer and dedicate each part of your body to God.

• Breathing. In order to be both relaxed and alert your breathing needs to be slow and deep, using the stomach muscles, not just breathing shallowly with your chest.

• Posture. If you are going to pray or meditate in one position for long, you should make sure that your back and neck are straight so that you can breathe freely and deeply, and that no limb is propping up another in an imbalanced way. The best position is sitting in a straight-backed chair with your feet flat on the floor and your hands in your lap. Standing or kneeling upright are also suitable positions, though you may find a prayer stool makes kneeling more comfortable.

USING A PRAYER STOOL

If you like to pray kneeling, but find it uncomfortable to kneel upright for long, try using a prayer stool. They are easy to make: all you need is a smooth plank about 18 inches long and 4 inches wide, supported at both ends so that it is about 5 inches off the ground (like a mini-bench). Kneel down and place this behind you so that it arches across your ankles. Place a cushion on it, then sit back onto the stool so that you are in a kneeling position with your back straight and your ankles tucked under the stool. This is a very helpful position for remaining relaxed and alert during prayer.

Posture and feelings affect each other

It is obvious that feelings affect, and are expressed by, the body. If embarrassed, you blush. In prayer and worship your feelings of joy, gratitude, anger, penitence, awe and love should be expressed with the whole of you, including your body. You might kneel in penitence; prostrate yourself in awe; dance with joy; cup your hands palm-upwards to receive from God.

However, it is equally true that your bodily posture affects your feelings, and your feelings affect your ability to pray and listen to God. If your body is relaxed, you will begin to feel more relaxed in mind and spirit. You can use your body to help you change negative feelings. For instance, if I know that I should repent of something but do not want to, then I make myself kneel in a crouched position. I have discovered that this posture gradually makes me feel more penitent. (You may find a different position helpful.) If I would like to praise God, but am feeling fed up or depressed, then I stand or move around with my arms raised and head up, perhaps singing. Generally I find that I begin to feel more like praising him! It is a deliberate physical act of obedience, part of 'offering your body as a living sacrifice' and God seems to honour it.

Walking and leaping and praising God

Spontaneous movement, alone or in a group of people with whom you feel relaxed, can deepen and enhance your worship. Play a recording of Christian songs, hymns, psalms or suitable instrumental music, and let your body express the music in simple movements. You could speak or record a prayer, poem or passage of scripture (eg the Lord's Prayer, the Magnificat or a psalm) and explore the meaning of each sentence or phrase in movement.

You will probably feel self-conscious and silly at first but, if you persevere, you will almost certainly find that expressing worship through movement is very liberating. It is entirely natural for both children and adults. In every other area of our lives we express joy, excitement, gratitude and love physically; with a hug, a burst of clapping or jumping up and down. Think of people watching their favourite sport! God has made us that way, so why do we assume that he wants us to be static, rigid and repressed in our worship? Paradoxically, it often seems to be the people who are shy or lacking in self-confidence, the elderly and those who have developed their intellects at the expense of their bodies, who come to find movement in worship most helpful. Gestures can express what words cannot.

Shout for joy to the Lord, all the earth

The Authorised Version of the Bible translates this verse from Psalm 100 as 'Make a joyful noise unto the Lord!' Using our voices is probably one of the most common physical expressions of worship. All the major revivals in the history of Christianity seem to have been accompanied by a burst of song writing. However, we are often rather narrow and habit-bound in our style of vocal worship. 'Making a joyful noise' does not just refer to hymns in church. Try singing praise to God on your own, in your prayer time, while walking, cycling, driving, washing up or in the bath. Try making up your own words or music. Setting a verse of scripture to a simple tune is a wonderful way of memorising it.

Speaking prayers aloud in church or in a small group is another way of obeying the injunction of Psalm 100. It also enables everyone to join in. Also many people find that praying aloud on their own (in suitable privacy!) can be very helpful in preventing their attention from wandering, and in making their intercession less woolly and more specific.

Those who have been given the spiritual gift of 'speaking in tongues' find it a helpful way of concentrating on God. It is not an uncontrollable ecstatic utterance, but simply speaking to God in an unknown language given by the Holy Spirit, which the speaker himself/herself does not understand. This requires considerable trust and obedience. James compares the tongue to the rudder of a ship – it is only a tiny part of the body but has a vital effect on the course of one's life. It is wild and restless: ' . . . no man can tame the tongue' (James 3:8). So of all the parts of the body, it is most important that the tongue is submitted to God and used to his glory.

By speaking or singing in tongues we express our willingness for the Holy Spirit to direct us wholly and to be the Lord of our speech.

Prayer walks

These can be done alone, or as a group who scatter and then meet to discuss and pray after the walk.

• Use the stations of the cross (a series of carvings or paintings telling the story of Good Friday) which you will find round the walls of most Catholic churches. Walk round and meditate in front of each one. Although the stations of the cross can be misused, you should find that, as a devotional aid, they help you appreciate more deeply the events recorded in the Bible.

• Walk in the countryside, praying. Use all your senses to explore, examine and enjoy God's creation. Thank him, and pray for farmers or about ecological issues, etc.

> In the winter, seeing a tree stripped of its leaves, and considering that within a little time the leaves would be renewed, and after that the flowers and fruit appear, he received a high view of the providence and power of God, which has never since been effaced from his soul. *Brother Lawrence*

• Go to a municipal rubbish tip. Walk over it, smell and touch things. Meditate on rejection and brokenness; on the way God re-uses and restores 'human rejects' and failures; on the biblical notion of Gehenna and hell. Pray about our wastefulness, and for people who live by scavenging.

• Go anywhere, and use it as a spur to prayer! As the seventeenth-century monk, Brother Lawrence, urges us (in his book *The Practice of the Presence of God*), work towards being aware of God wherever you are and whatever you are doing.

USING YOUR SENSES

> God ... richly provides us with everything for our enjoyment. *1 Timothy 6:17*

Our physical senses are amazing gifts from God and yet we tend to take them for granted unless they go wrong. Sight, hearing, smell, touch and taste are the ways in which we receive and take in from the world around us. Through them we learn discernment (being able to receive information and distinguish, for example, a red mug from a blue one, or the song of a skylark from a sparrow). Through the senses we receive warnings ('The toast is burning!' or 'That hurts!') We also receive tremendous pleasure in innumerable ways. (Try making a list of all your favourite sounds, sensations, sights, flavours and smells, thanking God for each one and for your body which enables you to enjoy them.) We also use our senses for establishing communication and relationships, with other people and with God. It is true that God does not 'touch' us in quite the same way as a friend's hug, but the creative use of our senses in prayer and worship can tremendously enrich our relationship with him. Here are a few suggestions.

- Sight

    Reflect on what it would be like to be blind. Think through some of your everyday actions step by step. How would they be affected? Thank God for your sight and pray for those who are blind.

    Use an object as a focus for meditation or a springboard for intercession – a candle, cross, flower, stone, seed, painting or photograph. Ask God what he wants to say to you through the object about you or about himself. In fact any object can be an aid to concentration and a way of broadening your prayer concerns. For instance, a bowl of sugar could spur you to pray for those who grow and sell it, for justice in the exploitative trading patterns between the West and developing countries, for dentists, for those who starve while we guzzle sweets, and so on!

    Have a go at drawing a simple diagram, picture, map or graph of your spiritual journey so far. You may well find that the Holy Spirit reveals new insights to you in the process. If you do this in a group, discuss in pairs what you have drawn.

- Smell

  Go on a sniffing expedition! Walk round your house or garden concentrating on how many different things you can smell. Try to become more aware of the richness of this gift, and thank God for it.

  Try using incense as an offering to God and an expression of your self-offering – it can be bought from most Catholic book shops or ecclesiastical suppliers. Study the many references to it in scripture. Psalm 141: 1–2 and Revelation 5:6–10 may be particularly helpful in using incense as a stimulus to prayer.

- Touch

  Become more aware of the incredible sensitivity of your skin. Try feeling things with your eyes shut. Explore different textures: cloth, fruit, walls, feathers, metal . . . Enjoy them, and pray for those with leprosy who have lost the sense of touch.

  In a group you could stand and hold hands at the end of a meeting, while you say the grace together or pray silently for the people on either side of you. If you are praying for a person who is ill or in need, several others could lay hands on him/her as they pray, and possibly anoint him/her with oil (James 5:14).

  For a bereaved or lonely person, holding their hand or giving them a hug will probably comfort them much more than words could do. Love should be the chief characteristic of our spirituality and touch can often be an appropriate way of expressing it.

- Hearing

  Look up in a concordance all the references to relevant words like 'ears', 'hear', 'listen', 'wait', etc. Study the ways in which God speaks to his people and the ways in which we do or do not hear and obey him. Try to spend more of your prayer time listening to God instead of talking at him.

  Lie flat on your back, breathe deeply and listen. First,

put your fingers in your ears and listen to the sounds inside your own body for a few minutes (heart, breathing, etc). Then listen to the noises inside the room. Finally, concentrate just on the noises from outside. This is a good pre-prayer exercise in relaxation and listening.

- Taste

Think of the amazing range of tastes that we can distinguish. Thank God for the rich variety of foods available to us through modern trade. Pray for the millions of people with inadequate or unvaried diets.

Arrange with a group of Christian friends for each member to prepare and bring to a meeting an item of food which expresses something about their life (or about your group or church, or about the topic you may have been studying together). Each person explains their contribution and then the group share the food together as an agape meal (see Acts 2:46; 1 Corinthians 11:17–34). Eating together is an ancient biblical expression of fellowship and shared faith.

EXPRESSING THE LORD'S PRAYER

Here are some suggestions for movements which can be used to express the meaning of the Lord's Prayer. These can be used kneeling, sitting or standing, and alone or with a group. (Of course it's even better if you create your own movements to prayer, psalms, etc. In the process you will come to understand more deeply what you are saying.) The italicised words in brackets give the meaning of the movements.

'Our Father in heaven . . . '

Head bowed and palms together, then slowly raise both. *(Your prayer and your attention rising towards God.)*

' . . . hallowed be your name . . . '

Open out your arms. *(Indicating the arc of heaven and your open-hearted praise.)*

' . . . your kingdom come . . . '

Bring hands down past your face to waist-level. *(God's rule over you is acknowledged first.)*

'. . . your will be done . . . '

Follow through movement with arms reaching out at waist-level. *(God's rule over the world.)*

'. . . on earth as it is in heaven . . . '

Drop your right hand *(pointing to the earth)*, then raise your left hand *(full span of God's rule).*

'. . . Give us today our daily bread . . . '

Bring your cupped hands slowly together with your palms upwards at waist-level. *(You are receiving with open hands.)*

'. . . Forgive us our sins . . . '

Bow your head and cover your face with both hands. *(Expressing your shame and penitence before God.)*

'. . . as we forgive those who sin against us . . . '

Bring your hands down and reach out to other people.

'. . . Lead us not into temptation . . . '

Raise your right arm in a defensive gesture across the face with your palm facing outwards.

'. . . but deliver us from evil . . . '

Bring your bent left arm up to form the vertical shaft of the cross. *(Expressing our deliverance from evil.)*

'. . . For the kingdom, the power and the glory are yours now and for ever. Amen.'

Open and raise your arms in praise.

MOVING ON

Learning that being human (with the physical body each of us has) is an asset, not a hindrance, to spiritual growth is a lifetime's task. It is important to start by getting our thinking right, and that is what this chapter is about. However, we must go on to discover for ourselves what 'physical spirituality' means: to try things out and experiment until we find what suits us. This is what the exercises which follow aim to enable us to do.

Day 1 'I am the bread of life'

• Get some coarse brown bread or a roll. (If you have time, you could make the bread yourself and stop at intervals to meditate on the ingredients and the process. This could also be done with a house group.)

• Read John 6:25–59. Then feel, smell and look carefully at the bread you have made, meditating especially on verse 35. Reflect on:

> Flour: grains ground down, and crushed. Apply this to Christ, yourself and the church.
> Yeast: how does a little 'yeast' of malice or wickedness spread in a person or group? (1 Corinthians 5:6–8; Matthew 16:8–12).
> Salt: 'You are the salt of the earth' (Matthew 5:13). How? Are you effective?
> Kneading: how does God pummel us into shape? Are you too soft and flabby, or too stiff and stodgy?
> Break the bread and eat some. How does Christ nourish you and satisfy your hunger? Pray that you may receive his feeding for today.
> Look at the remainder of the bread and read verse 33. Who can you share Christ's resources with today?

Day 2 'I am the light of the world'

• Read and meditate on John 1:1–9; 8:12; 9:5.

> For God who said, 'Let light shine out of darkness,' made his light shine in our hearts to give us the light of the knowledge of the glory of God in the face of Christ.   *2 Corinthians 4:6*

- Find or draw a map of the world, and place a lighted candle on top of the spot where you live. If possible, have the room in darkness. Hold up your hand close to the candle and see the flame shining through your fingers. Ask yourself whether Christ's light does shine through you. Is there anything in you which blocks his light?

- Place a lighted candle on a part of the world for which you want to pray. Ask that Christ's light may push back the spiritual, political, economic or social darkness there.

Day 3 'I am the gate for the sheep'

- Read John 10:1–10.

> ... we have confidence to enter the Most Holy Place by the blood of Jesus, by a new and living way opened for us through the curtain, that is, his body ...
>
> *Hebrews 10:19–20*

- Open the door of your room and position yourself so that you can make it the focus for your meditation.

- Reflect on the verses you have just read.

  What sort of 'gate' or 'door' is Christ?
  Do you imagine a great triumphal gateway, a humble narrow door, or an entrance made from the blood-stained wood of the cross? Think of the implications.
  Do you divide your time rightly between being inside and outside the fold?
  Do you have both Christian and non-Christian friends, and both church and non-church activities in a healthy balance? Pray about this.

- Close your door. Through Christ we are protected against Satan's attacks. Saved ... safe. Reflect on what it cost him. Thank him. Ask for his protection today.

Day 4 'I am the good shepherd'

- Read John 10:11–21 and reflect on it.

We all, like sheep, have gone astray, each of us has turned to his own way. . .   *Isaiah 53:6*

• Lie flat out on the floor, face downwards, with your arms spread out sideways. Think of occasions in your life . . .

when you have obstinately done things your own way and not listened to God or your conscience.
when you have 'stumbled' and fallen flat on your face.
when you have drifted away from God.
when you have felt alone and lost with no sense of purpose or direction.
when you have longed for someone who would love you for yourself and make you feel special.

You may need to repent of something, or ask God for healing of a painful memory.

• Curl up comfortably like a small child, on floor cushions or a sofa. Read Luke 15:3–7. Envisage yourself being held and cuddled by the Good Shepherd, safe in his strength and love. Relax and breathe deeply. Do you really believe that he would risk anything and sacrifice everything for your sake (and has done already on the cross)? Ask him to make you completely sure of it.

Day 5 'I am the resurrection and the life'

• Read John 11:17–44.

As for you, you were dead in your transgressions and sins . . . But because of his great love for us, God, who is rich in mercy, made us alive with Christ even when we were dead in transgressions . . .
                              Ephesians 2:1,4–5

• In order to identify with Lazarus, darken the room and lie down on your back, perhaps with a scarf or belt tied round your ankles, or a cloth wrapped round your body.

Do you believe that as a Christian, you are like Lazarus – a 'revived corpse'?

When and how did Christ call you into life?
Remember, and thank him for it.

• As Lazarus shuffled alive from the tomb, Jesus said, 'Take off the grave-clothes and let him go!' Many Christians are alive but still bound by the grave-clothes of old habits, desires, hurts and weaknesses.

What still binds you?
What binds your church?

Pray that the living Christ will set you free.

Day 6 'I am the way, the truth and the life'

• Read John 14:1–14 and meditate on it.

• Find a photograph of a friend or a member of your family who does not know or love Christ. Hold it in your hands.

How should you pray for this person in the light of Jesus' statement that 'no one comes to the Father except through me'?

Pray for this person and any others for whom God gives you a particular concern. Commit yourself to praying for them regularly.

Day 7 'I am the vine'

• Read John 15:1–17.

• If you have access to a vine, fruit tree, rose bush (or any other fruiting or flowering plant, though preferably one which requires pruning), go and look at it carefully. Use the plant as a focus for your prayer and meditation. If you have no plants, try to find a picture of a plant, or hold a piece of fruit in your hands.

• Reflect on John 15:1–3.

Have you allowed the Father to prune you and trim you clean?

Is there any 'dead wood' in your life, or in the structures of your church's life? Ask the Gardener to prune it so that it will bear more fruit.

- Reflect on John 15:5.

Do you believe Jesus' words, 'apart from me you can do nothing'?

To what extent do your actions stem from your own efforts and rely on your own strength and resources?

Do you truly remain in Christ and keep growing more closely attached to him?

What fruit are you producing? Is it 'fruit that will last' (v 16)?

- Spend some time in listening to God, and confession. Then cup your hands, palms upward, and ask to receive his forgiveness and resources.

9

MEDITATING ON SCRIPTURE

Deborah Seddon

If you think that meditation is for monks and nuns or clever people, or if you think that getting into the Bible is for scholars and preachers, you're wrong! Meditating on scripture is not a difficult intellectual exercise. It's more like thinking aloud in the presence of Christ.

WHAT IS MEDITATION?

We can handle the Bible in many different ways, some of which are dealt with in other chapters of this book. Let's look at four – Bible study, biblical criticism, meditation and contemplation – before homing in on meditation. That way we will see more clearly what meditation is, and what it isn't.

• Bible study is what it says: you study the text of the Bible as it stands in order to discover what it says, for example, about creation, or Solomon's temple, or what Jesus said about wealth, or what the doctrine of justification means. You can use various helps: reference Bibles, Bible dictionaries, concordances, commentaries. Bible study is primarily a thinking task, which then leads to personal action and spiritual response.

• Biblical criticism (which need not necessarily be destructive) means going behind the present text to ask questions like: How do we come to have this Gospel? What really happened at Jericho and Ai? What is the relationship between the books of Kings and Chronicles?

Beginning with the present text, we look for the original reading and meaning of the Greek and Hebrew text, using the literary, theological, archaeological and linguistic skills of detailed articles in learned journals, commentaries and scholarly text books.

• Meditation, like Bible study, means beginning from the text as it is, taking it as the word of God, and prayerfully and consciously seeking to be shaped and moulded by it. Although meditation and Bible study are different, we cannot make a sharp distinction; the one flows naturally into the other. However, whereas Bible study is primarily about understanding and about getting information from the scriptures, meditation is primarily about personal transformation and about letting the Bible get 'under our skin' so that we live it, breathe it and feel it.

• Contemplation is much more 'the look of love': a steady, deliberate, concentrated looking *to* God and *on* God, focusing on Jesus Christ in his life, death and resurrection. It is not concerned with asking questions or entering into debate. Rather, it is concerned with vision, praise, adoration and self-giving. Just as Bible study can flow naturally into meditation, so meditation can flow naturally into contemplation.

BE BALANCED!

We need to use the Bible in a variety of ways. We need the intellectual approach of study and criticism. We need to meditate and contemplate, if the wonder of God's work is to reach not only our heads but our hearts. However, if we're all meditation and no Bible study, we may lose the solid historical and objective realities of which the Bible speaks and drift off into a make-believe world of our own. Or, if we're all study and no meditation, we may stop at a dry academic analysis of the Bible text and never know an intimacy with the Lord who inspired it.

Let's look at the variety and balance which we need when using the Bible by exploring how four different pairs of eyes might view Mark 14:1–11. This is the story of the woman who anointed Jesus' head with very expensive perfumed ointment.

1 The Bible student will place the story in its context of the last week of Jesus' life, noting the preparation for Jesus' burial, the expensiveness of the ointment, the comments of the disciples. This is the stance of the cameraman or the artist who notes every detail of the scene.

2 The biblical critic will want to know about the relationship between the different Gospel accounts, and will compare Mark 14 with John 12. He will ask questions like 'Who was the woman?' 'Where did the event take place?' 'Are the accounts in Mark 14 and John 12 different from the story in Luke 7?' Here we have the investigative reporter and the literary critic at work.

3 The meditator enters into the story imaginatively and identifies with the various characters: with the woman's sacrificial devotion, the disciples' resentment, Jesus' appreciation, and the whole interlock of relationships. In meditation we want to be there and to find out: Where am I/are we in that scene? Our role here is that of reflective participants.

4 The person who contemplates will identify with the woman of whom Mark writes, and lavish all of him/herself (whether wealth, poverty, sin or love – or all!) on Jesus Christ with utterly unselfconscious extravagance. He or she approaches the passage with an attitude of worship.

HOW CAN I START?

Meditation is not a matter of techniques, of 'mind over matter'. We seek no automatic illumination. All we need is the right attitude – a 'humble and contrite spirit'. In coming to scripture, we recognise that it is *we* who need changing, not God. We believe that Jesus Christ is God's Word and the one to whom we are to be joined, and we trust the witness of the Spirit to lead us into the truth about ourselves, humanity and God.

However, given the right attitude, how do we move on? There are a thousand-and-one 'ways in' to meditation – ways in which we can allow God's word to become alive to us, to let it sink into us and become part of who we are. Some of those ways form part of the exercises at the end of this chapter. Focusing on key words, for example, is one way of getting inside a passage such as 1 John 4:7–12. If we stay with that passage for a while and dwell on the word 'love', we will come to see it as a multi-faceted diamond, sparkling with many lights. Some of those beams will illuminate us in a particular way, and the meditation will be a step in allowing God to re-shape us in his image. Personalising a text is another 'way in'. Romans 5:8, for example, may be so familiar that we cannot see it with fresh eyes in a Bible study; but if we say, 'God demonstrates his love for me in this: while I was still a sinner, Christ died for me', and then mull that thought over, we may open ourselves afresh to God's transformation.

Liturgy
Much church liturgy – such as the form of words used in the Anglican Church for Morning Prayer, Evening Prayer or Holy Communion – is close to the words of scripture from which it is derived. The regular use, for example, of parts of Psalms 95 and 96 in the Anglican service of Morning Prayer (where it's called the Venite) can be a scriptural meditation. We can learn to savour and appreciate the text and open ourselves to the hidden depths of its meaning. The repetition may at times seem boring, but it is repetition that shapes our minds and memories. And precisely because of its familiarity, different verses or phrases can frequently leap off the pages to inspire our thinking for the day.

Using liturgy as a basis for meditating on scripture has a long history. Tradition has it that St Augustine and St Ambrose composed the Te Deum in this way, each offering a line in turn ('You are God and we praise you: you are the Lord and we acclaim you . . . ') under the inspiration of the Spirit and from their store of memorised scripture – over sixteen hundred years ago.

Using rhythm

Repeating scripture rhythmically can be a way of both memorising and reflecting on the text. Monks and nuns did this in time past as they walked their cloisters: the practice was known as *ruminatio*, from the same root as our word 'ruminating' meaning both 'to chew the cud' and 'to meditate'!

Maybe you have no cloisters to walk round! So, why not try the route to the bus stop or station, or a local park or garden? Just take a single verse or a few words to mull over. 1 John 4:10, for example, is a text which lends itself to this kind of approach.

Sing it

Many of the new songs and choruses which have become part of church life in the last few years are, like much liturgy, close to, or even straight from, scripture. When you've a tune buzzing round in your head all day it can be irritating – particularly for those around you! If it's a scriptural song, why not take it as an opportunity for meditation? However, in your enthusiasm for new music, don't forget that poets and hymn writers have been doing the same thing for centuries! Don't cut yourself off from the scriptural hymns of past ages.

Write it down

Writing scripture down, as with the previous approach, is not just a way of learning scripture but of taking it slowly and so getting more out of each word, phrase or sentence. Try a psalm (eg Psalm 42) to see how this works. If you have skill in calligraphy (literally 'beautiful writing') why not produce something for display? 1 Peter 5:7 would be a good text. You may not be able to imitate *The Book of Kells*, but the process of producing it will allow you to meditate on the text, and it will be something you have created yourself!

Picture it

The Bible contains many pictures painted with words. Sometimes our meditation on the text can be aided by pictures that we know or scenes that we see. This can work two ways:

we may be struck by a picture or scene and link that with a Bible passage; or we may start with the Bible and move the other way. If you see a postcard or picture that makes a strong impression on you, take a minute or two to consider what aspects of it are touching you. Then, whether it is specifically a biblical theme or not, see whether any passages from the Bible come to your mind and let the picture you are looking at lead you into a brief reflection on the biblical connection. For instance, a news item about an accident at sea may bring into your mind the story of Jesus in the boat with the disciples during the storm (Matthew 8:23–27). The sight of a coffin may remind you about Jesus and the widow of Nain's son (Luke 7:11–17). A homeless travelling person may remind you of Jesus with nowhere to lay his head (Matthew 8:20).

Second, keep an eye open for the many everyday symbolic themes that recur through the Bible. Rivers, trees, stones, fire, bread, huge buildings, tiny rooms, the kitchen, shoes, clothes, books – all are full of biblical symbolism. A small concordance may help you here. It's possible to build up a rich canvas of meditation insights on the basis of a few simple items.

Finding time in a busy day

We often imagine that we have to have lots of time in order to meditate. This can be a matter of temperament. Some people do take longer to prepare themselves for prayer and meditation, where others can quickly jump in. However, meditation is more a matter of quality than quantity, and everyone can begin with an open Bible.

Even a mother on duty twenty-four hours a day can keep a Bible open in the kitchen (away from the spitting frying pan!), select a verse and return to it on and off during the day. As we reflect on a few passages, phrases or verses, they shape our waking, sleeping, living, thinking and feeling.

Making space for the Bible

Muslims often use a Qur'an stand on which to place the Qur'an in their homes. Perhaps Christians could begin to follow their example? The Bible is the world's best-seller, but hugely under-read and usually kept in a bookcase. Maybe it's time to leave it out on a table, as well as the flowers?

ADULTS ONLY?

Meditation sounds like a very 'grown-up' activity but it is not. In fact those with children have a head start (in some senses). Remember God's command to Israel:

> These commandments that I give you today are to be upon your hearts. Impress them on your children. Talk about them when you sit at home and when you walk along the road, when you lie down and when you get up. *Deuteronomy 6:6–7*

Children as young as three can begin to learn scripture (and enjoy it!). In dwelling on scripture they can meditate on it long before they know what the word 'meditate' means. Often, of course, it's children who teach adults: 'From the lips of children and infants you have ordained praise' (Psalm 8:2 and Matthew 21:16).

Here are a number of suggestions for a regular time together with your children.

• Take one verse and learn it together phrase by phrase. Select it according to the church season or from your own reading.

• Talk together about what it means. Listen to the children's wisdom.

• Make up a simple tune for the words so that you can sing them together. Share your embarrassment and pleasure.

• Write out the verse in pencil in the children's own books (a small plain-paper drawing book would be ideal), so that they can go over the lettering with felt pens and draw attractive borders or pictures to illustrate the text in their own way. (Older children will not, of course, need as much help.)

The key to meditation, whether we are on our own or in a group, whether we're nine years old or ninety, is that it is a discipline which is developed by practice. Find out what

161

suits you and stick with it. Grow with it. At the same time, don't limit yourself to only one system: you risk getting stuck in a rut. Let different ways of reading and responding to scripture challenge different areas and aspects of your life. This is what the following exercises aim to help you do.

Somehow we must find a way of remembering God that does not work in fits and starts, but that will actually last through the day; a kind of fundamental remembrance of God that will affect our heart, and allow our most unpremeditated and spontaneous behaviour to be transformed, as it were, at the root.

And this is, in fact, what meditation is supposed to achieve. It is not primarily a matter of spending a certain period of time every now and then having beautiful thoughts, but about building up a Christian memory . . . . Building up a Christian memory will unavoidably take time. It is a big mistake to look always for immediate results.

A Christian needs to have a Christian memory to allow him to deal with the unforeseen circumstances of his road too. Meditation can be seen as a kind of rehearsal for the unknown future; and the more diverse the material one has stored away in one's reserves, the better prepared one will be . . . . The basic point is that we need to be familiar with more doctrine than we actually require for immediate use, so that we will be prepared for whatever emergencies may arise . . . . So we need reserves, and that is the point of knowing one's doctrine, knowing one's Bible, knowing the lives and writings of the saints and the great theologians of the Church.

Meditation is more than acquiring knowledge. It is the forming of a mentality.   *Simon Tugwell*

TAKE SEVEN DAYS...

Day 1 A book – 1 Peter

This brief book lends itself to being read repeatedly. You can spend a number of months reading it as a whole, or stopping to 'live' in individual verses and immersing yourself in the text and in the Jesus Christ of whom it speaks. Heavenly revelation and insight is interwoven with the reality of earthly awareness. You can feel the sense of proportion, perspective and wisdom flowering from a life rooted in Christ. Even so, you may still feel that its brilliance eludes you. Here are some 'ways in' which could help you to meditate on this book. Start by reading through the whole book a number of times. It doesn't take long.

• Take 1 Peter 2:21–24 as the mid-point of the letter and trace themes from this crucial passage – suffering, living as strangers, salvation and hope, social behaviour – backwards and forwards through the letter.

> Follow through the repetition of any words or themes which strike you.
> Make up a tune for parts of key passages such as 1:3–5; 2:6–8; 4:12–13 .
> Write out 1:3–5 on art paper as an act of praise, and memorise it.

Turn some verses into prayer or praise by making some of the plural references singular: ' ... he has given *me* new birth ... ', 'Though *I* have not seen him, *I* love him ... ', ' ... for *I* am receiving the goal of *my* faith, the salvation of *my* soul'.

• If 1 Peter 2:13–14 or 3:17 make you angry, offer that anger to God in the spirit of 1:3 and 5:6. Let God know what you think and feel, and why, but allow God to be God and show you his perspectives. To make sure that you want to be shaped by scripture, ask yourself, 'Do I believe this? Do I live it out? How will this change me?'

Day 2 Varying the stress – Matthew 11:28

You can try this approach either with a passage that you know well but want to explore further, or with a passage that seems to say nothing but which you would like to work at. Simply take the verse and move the stress from word to word in turn and see what fresh insights the stress variation gives you.

'*Come* to me . . . ' (The simple invitation. Why do I resist?)
'Come to *me* . . . ' (It is Jesus calling me. Do I trust him?)
'Come to me, *all* . . . ' (Nobody is excluded, not even me.)

Continue in this way, allowing each word in turn to suggest its own questions or thoughts.

Day 3 Imaginative study – Deuteronomy 8

This meditative exercise is a kind of role play. You are to take the part of one of the thousands of Israelites on the borders of the Promised Land forty years after the exodus. You may need help from a commentary or Bible dictionary (or look at other bits of Deuteronomy, particularly chapter 1) in order to think yourself into the situation the Israelites were facing. Assemble your mental 'costume' first and then explore your situation.

• Reflect: you are in the desert with the Israelites.

Why has God brought you here?
How long have you been here?
What direction are you travelling in?
What descriptions of the desert (Deuteronomy 8:15) relate to your own experience?
Can you feel the hunger, thirst, dry mouth, cracking lips, sweat, threats?
Has God provided for you in any way? How?

• How do you want to commit yourself to the future with God? At the end of this exercise it would be good to return consciously to being you in the twentieth century. How does your meditation fit in with any of your present experiences, or those of others you know?

Day 4 Thematic study – trust

• Use a concordance to build up a series of verses which relate to your chosen theme – in this instance, trust. You can meditate on them in turn. Here are a set of Old Testament verses. You could look up New Testament ones to compare with them.

> Jeremiah 17:7–8, 'Blessed is the man who trusts in the Lord. He will be like a tree planted by the water that sends out its roots by the stream.'
> Proverbs 3:5, 'Trust in the Lord with all your heart . . . '
> Job 13:15, 'Though he slay me, yet will I hope in him . . . '
> Psalm 125:1, 'Those who trust in the Lord are like Mount Zion . . . '
> Isaiah 30:15, ' . . . in quietness and trust is your strength . . . '

In each case, look at the surrounding verses; see how they adds to your understanding. Then stay with the single line or two you have chosen to meditate on and digest, perhaps by asking yourself questions like: 'What would it be like if I really trusted God?' 'What is stopping me?'

Day 5 Old stuff – Exodus 26

Many parts of the Old Testament seem incomprehensible or irrelevant to many Christians. They feel either that Jesus has so 'fulfilled' the Old in the New that we needn't bother with the Old any more; or that we must read the Old symbolically or allegorically. These approaches have often been adopted in Christian history, but there are limits to them and we must think more creatively about scripture as a whole.

Here are a few ways in to meditating on Exodus 26. Take time to read through the whole chapter.

• The story of Israel is – not just was – essential to the story of Jesus.

• The movable tabernacle is just as important – if not more important – than the apparently more splendid temple of Solomon. John describes Jesus' presence on earth as a 'taber-

165

nacling' (John 1:14, usually translated 'dwelt' or 'lived'). Spend time mulling over this key word 'tabernacle'. Its meaning has many facets. Which strike you most?

• The sense of God's presence in the midst of his people – almost tangible and visible – is a vital theme of renewal in the Church today.

• Why is so much space given to details, here and elsewhere? Why is so much space given to details in your own life? The frequent repetition of tiny details (five of this or fifty of that) may at first sight seem trivial; but perhaps it is as we dwell on the repetition of little things that we can catch a vision of the splendour of the tabernacle, and of the God to whom it points.

• How far do you reflect the aspect of beauty – colour, pattern, shape – in your own life: in worship, in your home, in the world at large? A picture of the tabernacle in all its glory may, as we spend time with it, point us to the greater glory which is God's. (See also Revelation 21:11.)

• In theory the fulfilment of this passage is the presence of the Spirit in your personal, family and church life. What does this mean in practice? If we spend time imagining what it would be like actually to build the tabernacle (think of the thousands of fiddly ornate bits!), it may shed light on what 'building lives which glorify God' means, both individually and corporately.

Day 6 Meditation – John 13:1–9
The story about Jesus washing his disciples' feet is not simply about service. It is a picture of how God turns on their head our ideas of 'rights', authority and divinity. Read this account remembering that the death of Jesus is part of the picture too (see, for example, verse 8b).

• Spend time on John 13:1. It is very condensed. The themes of Jesus' origin, authority and destiny are repeated in verse 3. The scene is set for the whole event, both for the foot-washing and the death of Jesus.

• Move through the account slowly. Notice the movement and dialogue between one person and another: Judas (v 2), Jesus (vv 3–4), all the disciples (v 5), Peter (vv 6–9).

• Now put yourself in the place of each of the disciples in turn.

> How might you be in danger of being open to the devil?
> How do you receive Jesus?
> Why do you resist Jesus' ministry to you?

You will need to take time to answer each of these questions truthfully and then to offer all your responses to Christ in trust.

Day 7 Contemplation – John 13:1–9
Use the same passage as in the previous meditation, but this time be present as one of the disciples.

• Start from verses 1 and 3 again. Jesus ministers like this precisely because he has been given full authority (John 10:18).

• Look at Jesus, consider who he is and what he is doing. What Jesus Christ is doing – here and now, for you – is all that needs to sink in deeply. If your attention wanders, simply return again to where you got distracted and re-focus your attention. Jesus is humbling himself, ministering, washing, giving you a share of his life, dying for you. Receive that. Allow yourself to feel fully whatever you feel in response, but stay with your vision of God revealed in this act of Jesus.

• Bring to a close your time of what will have become worship.

> What is your final word to Jesus?
> What is his final word to you?

Hold these words in your heart.

• After a time of contemplation like this, you might want to rush into action immediately. It is quite important not to, although action must follow (vv 14,17). First, however, you need to discover in prayer how it should happen. This will give you something further to meditate on. You could use the same passage again, and ask questions like 'How can I extend to someone else Jesus' action for me?' Note who or what situations come into your mind.

> It is not knowing much, but realising and relishing things interiorly, that contents and satisfies the soul.
>
> I will ask God our Lord for what I want and desire ... Here it will be to ask for an intimate knowledge of our Lord, who has become man for me, that I may love him and follow him more closely. *St Ignatius*

10

DIRECTIONS FOR LIVING

Michael Botting

What motivates us to read a book? If we are going on holiday, we may like a detective thriller so that we can pit our brains and curiosity against Sherlock Holmes or Hercule Poirot. Or perhaps we have a fascination to know how other people have lived and prefer a biography. Or again, we may want to improve our knowledge of cooking or cars or classical music, so we take out a book from the public library. In every case the motivation will be obvious. What possible reason could we have for wanting to read the Bible?

CHANGE OR CHORE?
Paul's second letter to Timothy provides as succinct a reason as any:

> All Scripture is God-breathed and is useful for teaching, rebuking, correcting and training in righteousness, so that the man of God may be thoroughly equipped for every good work.   *2 Timothy 3:16–17*

We need to be sure that is actually what we want or Bible reading will simply be a duty, even a chore, to be got through as quickly as possible. There are a number of occasions in the Gospels when Jesus asked people who were obviously crippled in some way whether they wanted to be healed. We might have thought this was a stupid question, but Jesus knew healing would bring radical change. So let's be honest

169

with ourselves and about our spiritual healing. We will be in good company: the great early Father of the church, St Augustine of Hippo, in his more youthful days prayed: 'Give me chastity and continency – but not yet!' So, do we really want to be mature Christians 'thoroughly equipped for every good work'? It will bring lots of changes, challenges and responsibilities to our present way of life; but it will also bring exciting, new dimensions to our lives that those who don't read the Bible or apply its teaching won't know much about.

Most of us find reading the Bible difficult to get around to. There are at least three reasons why this is.

1   Sloth. We are all lazy, to some extent, and Bible reading requires some conscious effort. We will all no doubt agree heartily with the scripture that states, 'much study wearies the body' (Ecclesiastes 12:12).

2   Sin. We no doubt know enough about the Bible to know that it is going to challenge us to repent of our sins. Therefore we may hold back from reading because we are reluctant to change. A great American evangelist of the last century, D L Moody, used to say, and had written in the flyleaf of his Bible: 'This book keeps me from sin. Sin keeps me from this book'.

3   Satan. This name for the devil means 'adversary'. He is against all that God stands for, and therefore is especially concerned when anyone contemplates reading the Bible. It is instructive to notice how Satan dealt with our first parents in the Garden of Eden story (Genesis 3). Both clearly knew what was permitted and what was forbidden, yet three times Satan challenged them concerning God's word. He encouraged them to *doubt* God's word: 'Did God really say, You must not eat from any tree in the garden?' (v 1). He encouraged them to *disbelieve* God's word: 'You will not surely die' (v 4). He encouraged them to *disobey* God's word: 'God knows that when you eat of it your eyes will be opened, and you will be like God, knowing good and evil' (v 5).

Jesus warned that Satan's ways do not change (John 8:44–46), so we can expect him to encourage *us* to doubt,

170

disbelieve and disobey the Bible too. If we are to overcome the things that stop us reading the Bible, we'll need some positive encouragement!

WHY READ THE BIBLE?

> The people of the Bible, within its own time and particular situation, raised the same questions and tried to answer them ... There are many – we Christians – who believe that the road that was followed by that people is the right road, the way of God. That is why Christians ... read the Bible as an indispensable contribution to their reflection; to help them in their analysis of reality and in their search for answers to the questions that life itself raises. They see the history of the people of the Bible as a kind of model for action that hit the mark and that has God's warranty. That is why Christians study the Bible; not just to learn what happened way back then, but also, and above all, in order to know, through information received from the Bible, in a better way, the meaning and importance of what's happening today, all around us, in our own history. *Carlos Mesters*

The scriptures have messages in three tenses.

• We look *back* to read how God has revealed himself in history, and supremely in Jesus Christ: 'in these last days he has spoken to us by his Son' (Hebrews 1:2). The primary purpose for the writing of John's Gospel was that we might find faith and new life in God's Son: 'these are written that you may believe that Jesus is the Christ, the Son of God, and that by believing you may have life in his name' (John 20:31).

• We are encouraged to look *forward* in hope of the glorious future that God has planned for all those that love him: 'For everything that was written in the past was written to teach us, so that through endurance and the encouragement of the Scriptures we might have hope' (Romans 15:4; see also 1 Corinthians 2:9 and Ephesians 1:3–23).

• The *present* is the time for obedience, which has a much larger place in the Bible than is commonly supposed. In the New International Version Concordance the word 'obey' and derivatives like 'obedience' and 'obedient' appear in over 250 texts. Yet it is disobedience that figures so prominently in the lives of many of the people whom the Bible tells us about, often with disastrous consequences: the fall of mankind occurred because mankind was disobedient; so did the flood in the time of Noah; and the exile of Judah to Babylon, despite frequent warnings from prophets like Jeremiah; Saul, the first king of Israel, lost his kingdom because he failed to obey God; Jonah had a very confining problem in a large fish because he was very clearly told by God to go and preach to Nineveh but went in exactly the opposite direction.

By contrast one of the great kings of the Old Testament, Josiah, having discovered the law of the Lord (probably the book of Deuteronomy) in the temple, immediately had its precepts obeyed. When Jesus was being tempted in the wilderness by Satan, he repeatedly responded, to the temptations with, 'It is written ... ' followed by a quotation from the Old Testament. In his teaching he tells of two men building the 'houses' of their lives on 'rock' or 'sand' (Matthew 7). When each house was tested by wind, rain and flood the house on the rock continued to stand, whereas the house on the sand failed the testing because the man who built it did not obey. It should be no surprise, therefore, that Paul writes to Timothy, as we have seen, reminding him that the inspired writings of scripture are: ' ... useful for teaching, rebuking, correcting and training in righteousness'. Hearing God's word and acting on it is the key to real life.

FAITH AND OBEDIENCE
However, surely the heart of the gospel is not about keeping rules but that salvation comes through repentance of sin and exercising faith in Jesus Christ alone? Didn't Jesus begin his ministry with that very message (Mark 1:15)? Didn't Peter conclude his great Pentecost sermon with the call that each hearer turn away from his sin and be baptised in the name of Jesus Christ (Acts 2:38)? Didn't Paul write to the Galatians

that if a person is put right with God through the law, it means that Christ died for nothing (Galatians 2:21)? Yes, all that is true. So how does obedience to God's law fit in with the good news of God's salvation which is so freely available to us?

Salvation comes through obedience!
Scripture teaches that whoever 'does these things [ie keeps the law] will live by them' (Galatians 3:12). The catch, however, is that only one man in history has fulfilled that requirement, namely Jesus. He, therefore, had no need to die and could have been translated to heaven at his transfiguration. Everyone else has broken the law and therefore cannot get to heaven if keeping the law is the only way! It is because Jesus Christ chose deliberately the way of disfiguration, to go the way of the cross, all who repent and believe in him can receive eternal life.

The law shows our need
A person who once attempted to teach me to play the piano used to say that going to piano recitals or hearing great piano concertos inspired her to practice at her own piano playing with much greater enthusiasm, except when she heard one virtuoso, Claudio Arrau. His playing was so brilliant that it always filled her with despair. If that was the standard, what was the use? Paul's teaching in Romans 7 is much the same concerning right living. When he realised what the law's demands were, he felt like packing up and throwing in the sponge. The commandments of God were holy, right and good, but they showed the great apostle up for being terribly sinful. However, all was not lost. The commandments also caused him to seek salvation another way, through faith in Jesus Christ. So towards the end of Romans 7 (v 24) Paul wrote: 'What a wretched man I am! Who will rescue me from this body of death? Thanks be to God – through Jesus Christ our Lord!'

Obedience is evidence

Obedience to God's law is not – for you and me – a way in which we are put right with God. God's law shows us, in fact, that we can't get right with God by ourselves. However, having been saved by God, the law of God really comes into its own. Once we belong to God's family, we will want to know God's law and obey it – to read the Bible for instruction as to how to live, not out of duty or as a chore, but out of love for our heavenly Father. Three passages in the New Testament illustrate how and why we should be hearing God's word and obeying it.

• John 15:9–17. Jesus showed how much he loved his Father by obeying him totally. This is surely true of all love relationships. Spouses show their love for each other by doing what is known to please the other. The same should be true between children and parents. Jesus asks his disciples to show love for him by doing what he says. Our obedience is not in any way an attempt to earn our salvation, which we already have by faith. It is simply evidence for Jesus, ourselves and the watching world that we love him.

• James 2:14–24. If we have faith in Christ for salvation, it will inevitably be shown by a changed life. This will sometimes mean taking practical social action. If we see someone clearly in need – perhaps of food and clothes – and only wish them well without doing anything to provide them with the physical necessities of life, what evidence is there of faith in Christ?

A work with which I was very much involved for twelve years of my ministry is that of St George's Crypt in Leeds. One of my predecessors as vicar was Don Robins who, during the industrial depression of the 1930s, had hungry, ill-clothed, dejected men all round the church, unable to get work and ashamed to go home penniless. How could Robins claim he loved Christ and ignore the plight of these men? So, greatly daring, he opened up the crypt of the church, which for years had been the burial place for some 750 people, and began to use it as a centre at which those in need could find practical help. And that work still continues to this day.

• Matthew 25:31–46. In this awesome and challenging parable about the final judgement, the Son of Man separates people into two groups, as a shepherd might separate sheep from goats, the righteous on his right and the others on his left. The evidence for being a genuine believer will be how we have behaved and, in particular, how we have shown practical love for our neighbour, thereby showing our love for Jesus. We read the same lesson in John's letters: 'And he has given us this command: Whoever loves God must also love his brother' (1 John 4:21). So Jesus expects us to show practical love to our fellow human beings by feeding the hungry, clothing the naked, caring for the sick and visiting those in prison. In doing this for others we are, in fact, doing it for him.

HELP FROM THE BIBLE

The Bible may provide plenty of instruction in how to live; and hearing God's word and obeying it may be the path to a full life. But how do we get down to doing something about it? We need help! And help is just what the Bible offers.

Bible motives

• Obedience brings true happiness. Psalm 1 says, 'Blessed is the man who does not walk in the counsel of the wicked or stand in the way of sinners or sit in the seat of mockers. But his delight is in the law of the Lord, and on his law he meditates day and night.'

Contrary to what Satan tempts us to believe, God is no killjoy. Psalm 1 is by no means the only psalm to stress how God longs to bless us: 'Open wide your mouth and I will fill it' (Psalm 81:10); 'For the Lord God is a sun and shield; the Lord bestows favour and honour; no good thing does he withhold from those who walk is blameless' (Psalm 84:11).

In the New Testament Jesus assures us that those who hunger and thirst after righteousness will be satisfied and blessed. And part of the fruit of the Spirit is joy.

• Obedience brings true freedom. Jesus said to those who believed in him, 'If you hold to my teaching, you are really my disciples. Then you will know the truth, and the truth will set you free' (John 8:31–32).

The idea that being chained to Jesus is the way to find freedom seems absurd, yet is in fact true. It's part of the paradox of the gospel: we must die in order to live! But the freedom that comes through obedience to God is in fact the deepest and truest freedom – the freedom to be fully human. As one of the prayers in the Anglican *Alternative Service Book* puts it: 'O God . . . to know you is eternal life, to serve you is perfect freedom'.

We must not confuse freedom with licence. The only way that we can enjoy freedom on our roads, for example, is if we all obey the Highway Code. When we don't, there is chaos and frequently death. Even in the Garden of Eden God put limits on which fruit our first parents were permitted to eat. Attractive though total licence may seem, we would soon find ourselves imprisoned by it. If you are an enthusiast for orchestral concerts, you may admire the marvellous freedom and control some great concert pianist shows as he or she plays some great concerto. How is this inspiring music achieved? Quite simply, it is because the pianist lives a disciplined life of regular piano practice. Jesus calls us to a similar discipline, that the world may be amazed at the freedom and control of our lives and want to know our secret.

• Obedience also brings assurance of salvation. In 2 Peter the apostle writes of how we can have magnificent assurance of our salvation. In fact, as we shall see, this assurance is something which grows as we live disciplined and obedient lives.

> His divine power has given us everything we need for life and godliness through our knowledge of him who called us by his own glory and goodness. Through these he has given us his very great and precious promises, so that through them you may participate in the divine nature and escape the corruption in the world caused by evil desires.
>
> For this very reason, make every effort to add to

your faith goodness; and to goodness, knowledge; and to knowledge, self-control; and to self-control, perseverance; and to perseverance, godliness; and to godliness, brotherly kindness; and to brotherly kindness, love. For if you possess these qualities in increasing measure, they will keep you from being ineffective and unproductive in your knowledge of our Lord Jesus Christ. But if anyone does not have them, he is shortsighted and blind, and has forgotten that he has been cleansed from his past sins.

Therefore, my brothers, be all the more eager to make your calling and election sure. For if you do these things, you will never fall, and you will receive a rich welcome into the eternal kingdom of our Lord and Saviour Jesus Christ.   *2 Peter 1:3–11*

Obedience gives us that confidence that we really belong to God as his redeemed children. It opens up our minds to the truth and sets us free to enjoy a foretaste of the glorious liberty of the children of God, which we shall experience in all its fullness in heaven (Romans 8:21).

So the Bible can motivate us to dig deeper, to find out what God says and to obey. If we long for happiness, freedom and an assurance that we do indeed belong to God, then we will only find these things if we seek them indirectly – and seek first God's kingdom.

The Holy Spirit

When Jesus was tempted by the devil in the desert at the very beginning of his ministry, we are told particularly that he was led there by the Spirit. When the temptations came, he was able to recall the scriptures (which he had obviously studied from his youth so he knew what was right living) and he was able to resist the temptations in the power of the Holy Spirit. We thought earlier of how the apostle Paul, when he read of what the law required of him, felt condemned because he knew he was a slave of sin (Romans 7). However, Paul goes on to write of the work of the Holy Spirit in the life of the believer.

> Those who live according to the sinful nature have their minds set on what that nature desires; but those who live in accordance with the Spirit have their minds set on what the Spirit desires. The mind of sinful man is death, but the mind controlled by the Spirit is life and peace ...
>
> *Romans 8:5–6*

Paul writes in much the same way to the Galatians (5:16–25). We live in a spiritual environment in which every impulse to hear God's word and obey it will be challenged. Living rightly for God won't come easily! However, if we have faith in Jesus Christ, then we also have the gift of his Holy Spirit who we can call upon to enable us to rise above our natural temptations, and so to be obedient and live rightly. As Paul says, 'Since we live by the Spirit, let us keep in step with the Spirit' (Galatians 5:25).

The Bible points the way

The ten commandments have not been repealed, though they obviously have to be culturally reinterpreted for Western society. Most of us are not sorely tempted to desire our neighbour's cattle or donkeys unless we live in deep rural areas, but we may covet his Volvo. If we are to know what God is like and what pleases him, then we will need to see what the Bible has to say. This may require the discipline of Bible study if we are to apply the commandments to our lives today and if we are to draw biblical principles for right living from the many stories in the Bible.

The Bible warns of pitfalls. When people say the Bible is out of date, they reveal only too clearly that they have not read it. It would be difficult to find a more topical passage than Proverbs 5 – a warning against adultery – and no doubt it has been topical in every generation since it was written.

Jesus also warned in the Sermon on the Mount of the consequences if we persist in sin. He took several of the Old Testament commandments and showed that it was not only the letter but the spirit of the law which had to be obeyed. If we are to know what not to do, then we will need more than common sense: we will need the discipline of getting to grips with God's word and seeing what it has to say.

USING THE BIBLE

So reading the Bible for instruction in right living seems like a good idea! With the help of God the Holy Spirit, we can delve into God's word and begin to see the signposts pointing the way ahead. He will help us, too, in the nitty-gritty details of obedience to God in daily life. This is a long-term spiritual discipline which leads to freedom, fullness and true happiness. But before you open your Bible, here are a few simple guidelines to help you.

• Try to read the Bible regularly, systematically and responsibly: *regularly*, because most people find that routine, whether in jogging or Bible reading, helps us to be disciplined; *systematically*, because, if we just stick with the bits we like and know, we will build a God in our own image; *responsibly*, because truth is important and we must one day give account of how we have used it. As you read, ask the questions which a look at 2 Timothy 3:16 encourages us to consider the following:

> What truth is being taught here?
> What error is being rebuked?
> What faults need correcting?
> What instruction is given to promote right living?

In our meditation we ponder the chosen text on the strength of the promise that it has something personal to say to us for this day and for our Christian life, that it is not only God's Word for the Church, but also God's Word for us individually. We expose ourselves to the specific word until it addresses us personally. And when we do this, we are doing no more than the simplest, untutored Christian does every day; we read God's Word as God's Word for us.

We do not ask what this text has to say to other people. For the preacher this means that he will not ask how he is going to preach or teach on this text, but what it is saying quite directly to him. It is true that to do this we must first have understood the content of the verse, but here we are not expounding it or preparing a sermon or conducting Bible study of any kind; we are rather waiting for God's Word to us. It is not a vacuous waiting, but a waiting on the basis of a clear promise. Often we are so burdened and overwhelmed with other thoughts, images and concerns that it may take a long time before God's Word has swept all else aside and come through. But it will surely come, just as surely as God himself has come to men and will come again. This is the very reason why we begin our meditation with prayer that God may send his Holy Spirit to us through his Word and reveal his Word to us and enlighten us.

Dietrich Bonhoeffer

• You may find it helpful to keep a special note book and write down what you have learnt from your reading. This will help you to be quite specific in applying the Bible. (See the last chapter of this book for more on journalling.)

• Pray through what following God is going to mean in your life today and in the future.

• Obey!

TAKE SEVEN DAYS ...

'Reading the Bible for instruction in right living' is a lifetime's work! In the seven studies which follow we can only look at a few general issues, in particular that of actually doing something about what we hear.

Day 1 Choose your friends carefully

• Read Proverbs 1:7–19. This passage may portray an extreme example of being led astray by friends, but the principle holds true. It's easy to be swept along by others and to live life in such a way that we blend in with our surroundings. We may not have received much wisdom from our earthly parents, but here we are presented with wisdom from our heavenly Father.

Jesus says to us, as he said to his disciples, 'Follow me.' The quality of obedience which that demands will become impossible if we allow the world to 'squeeze us into its own mould' (Romans 12:2, J B Phillips). So, although we are to be *in* the world (it is neither possible nor desirable for things to be otherwise), we are not to be *of* the world. We should be swimming against the stream, not floating with the current.

• Have you been swept along with the world's way of doing things? Do you go with the world in stealing public property because 'everybody else does'? Should you be repenting of a form of indirect dishonesty? Pray over these questions.

• How will you answer the cry of, 'Come along with us' whether it be a call from society at large or from particular people? What practical steps can you take: for example to make sure you are not holding onto anything obtained dishonestly?

Day 2 'Listen to me'

• Read Proverbs 1:20–33. Here we have a contrast between the evil suggestions of violent men in Proverbs 1:7–19 and the appeal of wisdom personified. Notice that wisdom's voice is public, whereas the voice of the evil men is undercover. Jesus, the incarnate Word and Wisdom of God, said 'Light has come into the world, but men loved darkness instead of light because their deeds were evil' (John 3:19). Hearing God's word places us in a privileged and responsible position. Refusing to respond is not a position of neutrality but the path of decay and degeneration leading, ultimately, to disaster.

• Maybe you have often heard God's voice speaking what you have known to be wisdom, have ignored it, and failed to allow your life to be changed. Pray about this.

• What steps are you going to take to make sure your Bible reading is regular, systematic and responsible, so that God's voice has a chance to get through to you? Have you opened a special note book in which to write down what you have learnt?

Day 3 'Trust me!'

• Read Proverbs 3:1–20. The heart of this passage is a call to trust in the Lord (v 5). If we do so, we know he will direct our lives. We can also give confidently of our possessions because he will ensure we have all we need. Whereas the world seeks and worships money, those who live rightly discover there is greater profit in seeking and worshipping the Lord.

• The Lord corrects those he loves (Hebrews 12:6). Do you need correcting concerning your lack of faith in him in the very practical affairs of daily living? Pray about this.

• Do you tend to be anxious about many things, especially concerning money and guidance? What action are you going to take next time you are tempted not to trust the Lord in some way?

Day 4 Social security

• Read Proverbs 3:21–35. The media keeps us constantly informed about the very real insecurities of life. We must use our God-given wisdom to take reasonable precautions against unnecessary problems. But, having done that, we can commit our lives and those of our loved ones into the Lord's hands and sleep soundly.

In loving our neighbour it is not enough that we do him no harm (v 29), but also that we do him positive good (v 27).

• Have you been sufficiently concerned for the future without being anxious about it? Pray about this.

• In what practical ways can you help those in need? What possessions do you have (say of clothes) that you have not used for ages, that you could give away to those in need?

Day 5 Do we ever forget what we look like?

• Read James 1:19–27. This passage really sums up all that we have seen so far, so much so that you might wonder why it has been selected. But isn't that our trouble? We are constantly hearing the Lord's word to us but we persistently do nothing. If we looked in a mirror and saw a dirty face, we would take action at once.

• Pray: 'Speak, Lord, for your servant is listening' (1 Samuel 3:9–10).

• If you are persistently not listening to what the Lord is saying through the scriptures, your conscience, the church and your personal circumstances, ask yourself, 'Why?' What must you do? Perhaps we need to have a prayer partner or 'soul friend' with whom we can share openly and honestly, because it is so easy to be blind to our own faults. Someone with whom we really could confide in complete confidence could help us get our blinkers off.

Day 6 Prejudice

• Read James 2:1–13. One of the people who was helping at St George's Crypt some years ago dressed up like a tramp and attended a Christmas tree service in a very respectable church. He was very obviously shunned and encouraged to sit in a seat well away from most of the congregation. There was considerable embarrassment when the preacher spoke of how Jesus became poor, and then illustrated his sermon by calling the 'tramp' to come forward. Would the church of which you are a member have behaved any differently?

• Are you prejudiced or discriminating about class, colour or sex? How can you repent of and correct anything which is amiss? Pray about this.

• To what extent do you look out for visitors that come to your church? Or do you just mix with your regular clique? Would you treat someone who shares your background differently from someone who isn't like you?

Perhaps your church needs friends from another church to give constructive criticisms of the way you welcome strangers. 'All one in Christ Jesus' (Galatians 3:28) should describe our churches.

Day 7 Mind your language!

• Read James 3:1–12. During the Second World War, Britain was stirred on to victory by the inspiring speeches of Winston Churchill. The country was also being constantly warned that 'careless talk costs lives'. In spiritual warfare, too, the tongue is an all important member. You could say that God has chosen the tongue to change lives through the proclamation of the gospel, and Satan has chosen the tongue to ruin lives by careless talk.

• Do you need to be honest with yourself over the use of your tongue, perhaps especially over gossip and our 'economy with the truth'? 'Gossip is so tasty – how we love to swallow it' (Proverbs 18:8, GNB). Pray about this.

• Which side is your tongue on in spiritual warfare? If both, what action are you going to take to bring it under control?

> Do not merely listen to the word, and so deceive your-selves. Do what it says.   *James 1:22*

11

SPIRITUALITY AND POLITICS

Alison White

A DIRTY WORD

Politics has become a dirty word and many Christians have difficulty with it. How many times have you read or heard someone say, 'The church should keep out of politics'? We have come to believe this is true. Politics should happen in parliament and in the newspapers; 'they' should be allowed to get on with it; it is a matter for the experts. We have narrowed it down in such a way that we feel justified in allowing ourselves to think we are not involved.

> I am puzzled about which Bible people are reading when they suggest religion and politics don't mix.
> *Archbishop Desmond Tutu*

Fear of politics has a long history in Christianity. Christians have rightly struggled with trying to be a holy people and, for many, the obvious way to achieve or preserve holiness is to stay clear of anything that might tarnish it. The realm of politics has been a fabled land full of the ogres of compromise, deceit, and – the biggest enemy of all – worldliness. For some, Christian identity is threatened when Christians have to move too far outside the immediate circle of the church and become involved in a world where a strand of theology tells them they do not belong. There have always been exceptions and Christian men and women who have been part of the political process. Some of them the church has done its best, at least retrospectively, to admire and keep in its prayers.

The majority of Christians have favoured banishing political discussion from the pulpit or study group for fear that different opinions would clash and unity would be destroyed. These are real fears. In healing them, rather than avoiding them, Christians are brought to face questions about what and who they believe about God and the world, and about their own place in it all.

At the outset some of the dirt needs scraping off the word 'politics' so that it can be liberated from narrow definitions and understood in a more positive way. It may then provide a new dynamic for our spiritual lives.

Politics is about how human beings live together in society. It concerns how they organise themselves to meet needs which cannot be dealt with by an individual. It is about how they deal with resources and power, and behave towards one another. This broad understanding of politics gives each of us room to see that we are involved after all. Politics is about *us* – not a separate world.

WORLDS APART

'The earth is the Lord's, and everything in it,' declares Psalm 24. The congregation may well agree but when asked to meditate on the world, God's creation, will turn only to the beauty of nature. The natural world supplies us with rich images of the Creator – the awesomeness of his fertile imagination, the sheer wonder of what he has made. It gladdens our eyes and nurtures our spirits. Yet the psalmist wrote that *everything* is the Lord's, not only the beautiful and uplifting parts. We have become proficient in separating out the things that we think are proper concerns for God and ignoring the rest.

The whole world, moreover, is the object of God's love. His commitment is passionate and total and is not primarily for the church or the righteous. The God who made the world cannot leave it be nor does he discriminate about which parts he will love. This is part of the scandal of our faith.

Human life is generally more comfortable if it can be divided up into compartments. Divisions are made between private and public life; between mind, body and spirit; between world and church. A sense of what is appropriate to each is developed and this frees us from some of the more difficult questions and tensions. There is a pressing need to recover a sense of wholeness.

People feel more competent in some areas than in others. The temptation that follows is to deny or to limit involvement in spheres that seem alien to us. Even for the quietest and most retiring member of the human race there are three main areas in which he or she will live. The first is the obvious one of personal development, growth in understanding and maturity, of being 'who I am'. This is not just an interior matter, it will affect an individual's behaviour. The second area is that of the local community, which will include family, the place and people where we live, where we work and any group with which we are associated. The third area is more difficult to define and is made up of the complex structures and systems in which our lives are involved. For example, when we shop in a supermarket, we think no further than the meals to be provided. We do not generally consider the means by which the products arrived on the shelves, the selection of goods, the destination of the profits, the working conditions of the employees. We feel we have little control or say over these matters and yet at the same time we are happy to profit by them.

God made me a whole person, living in a particular society in the world. I am not free to say that in this or that area I am a Christian but in this one I am just a citizen. Being a Christian affects the whole of our lives, corporate as well as individual. It becomes more difficult, then, to say that politics has nothing to do with spirituality.

'I AM WITH YOU'

When that scrap of a baby was born in Bethlehem, everything changed. In an outrageous kind of way God was saying, 'I am with you.' We had lived as though we saw God through a telescope, believing him to be far away, removed from earthly concerns. He might send instructions, even messengers, but to take our human flesh is surely taking commitment

187

to extremes. God has met us in Jesus on our terms and his, as man and God. He is part of our history not just our philosophy.

The implications of this incarnation turn everything around. Our spirituality is moulded by that of Jesus himself, our mind shaped by his. 'Your attitude should be the same as that of Christ Jesus,' says Paul in Philippians 2:5, and goes on to remind us of the total self-giving of Jesus for us. Faith does not remove us from the world. It plunges us right in, to take risks and to be vulnerable. The challenge to us in what we have called political spirituality is the challenge of 'God with us'.

Jesus is our model. He takes us out of the business of theory – even out of our churches – to be in our communities, to know people, to be involved beyond our own circle. Often, because we are frail, we will get it wrong, misunderstand, patronise, lose courage or prefer our own interests. Then we, too, need to know that the same Jesus is with us so that we can begin again.

> Those who profess the religion of Jesus must bring into
> public life and into the legislature the stern, practical,
> social, real side of the Gospel. The religion of Christ
> must become again what it was when He was on earth.
> *Josephine Butler, 1828–1906*

It is a costly adventure; the cross stands as a stark reminder of this. A price has to be paid for resisting all that makes human beings less than they were meant to be. Jesus was not in the business of comforting those who were pushed out of society, or giving ointment to the sick or appeasing those in power. His life was given to see people changed in themselves and in their social relationships – to see the kingdom come.

YOUR KINGDOM COME

Where would you look for the kingdom of God? The answer to this question is an important point on the compass for our spiritual journey.

Some will answer, 'It is inside us.' The kingdom (or rule) of God has become a personal, interior matter. We are travelling towards personal peace and an inner experience of God. Others will say, 'It is in the church.' In this case we are left with the danger of a barrier between the church and the world, and the feeling that retreat is the best course of action. Some will point to the future for the coming of the kingdom, which in turn implies that it has nothing to do with any society on earth. The problem with this is that it leads to the feeling that one need not be greatly concerned with what society is like. What really counts is the eternal kingdom when all this earthly muddle will be behind us.

All these points of view have substantial elements of truth in them, but even put together they miss the force of Jesus proclaiming, 'The kingdom of God is at hand.' This is the main theme of Jesus' ministry, which had been heralded in the Old Testament. The kingdom is about a new way of living. Here is found the true shape for human society which would transform the face of the earth. It reveals in our world the character and concerns of God.

The kingdom is good news precisely because it is God's kingdom and not another human scheme. It is a challenge to all those who hear, 'Today the kingdom has come near you.' It is a call – to faith, to change, to repentance, to commitment to the radically new way revealed in and by Jesus.

One of the consequences of the kingdom will be a transforming of values and the way we see the world. The beatitudes and the parables of the kingdom are so familiar that they have lost their power to shock us. Nonetheless, they stand the 'I-come-first' world on its head.

The values of the kingdom will often make the Christian community an uncomfortable one for the rest of society. The presence of the kingdom will question the motivation and goals of many schemes. It will, for example, reveal inadequate understandings of justice and abuses of authority. It means that we cannot simply identify Christianity with a particular political party or even a culture. God's design is far greater than we could devise. There are many attractions and false securities in settling for a Christianity which fits in with the mainstream of the society in which it is present. It is all too easy for Christians to believe that issues they hold dear are also God's prime concerns. It is God's kingdom, not ours. It calls for clear-sightedness and courageous faith to be part of what God is doing and to accept the responsibility he gives to us.

> A stable situation is not necessarily a peaceful one; injustice, exploitation and discrimination are incompatible with real peace; and so a peace-directed person may be the one on whom it is laid to rock the boat, challenge the system.
> *Jo Vellacott*

RESPONSE AND RESPONSIBILITY

Spirituality is, at its heart, the expression of our response to God. His character, concerns and activity shape our own. As we encounter him more fully, so our response will grow. We are dealing with a God who is both inffinite and found in the form of a man from Nazareth. Our God is involved in the most intimate working of our personal lives and loves the world in all its complexity. Political spirituality is one way of describing our response to the God who is beyond our individuality.

Christians, not surprisingly, find this kind of God disquieting. This is too much like hard work. We prefer the Holy Spirit to come to us as a comforter rather than as a disturber. He may, 'convict . . . [of] sin and righteousness and judgment' (John 16:8), but only on a personal level. Religion has become a private practice. We need a renewed experience of the Spirit as an unsettler of our values.

Our response to the Spirit who lives within us means becoming communities of faith, which, like the Spirit, also challenge and disturb the social order. This is to take up our prophetic role, proclaiming in word and action the values of the kingdom which challenge the *status quo*. In such a risky enterprise we must constantly seek a vision of God in our prayer and contemplation.

One of the uncomfortable gifts God has given to human beings is that of responsibility. It is intrinsic to our humanity. At the beginning, God gave a very good creation into the hands of men and women. He has not changed his mind.

PARISH OF WYNBERG, CAPE TOWN, SOUTH AFRICA

In the years before the ending of apartheid in 1994, there were many moving examples of Christians in South Africa who were working and praying to see justice in their land. In mid-1986 a substantial part of the black township of Crossroads, just outside Cape Town, erupted in violence. The state police, rather than restoring order, were seen to be aiding and abetting one side in the conflict. Many people who had lived in the area were made homeless.

Faced with this crisis the people of Wynberg parish knew they must respond. They opened the church halls and buildings and welcomed in the refugees in the name of Jesus. Church members found all kinds of ways to be involved, offering time, money, clothes, and food. This was not the first time the parish had been involved in such activity. It began in 1977 when they opened their doors to those left without shelter when the shanties in Rodderdam were demolished.

It was more than an act of compassion. The action meant a deliberate decision to break the law in the shape of the Group Areas Act, which designated which race might live in which area. This experience, which brought much heart-searching to the parish, also faced the Christian community with the implications of being God's people in South Africa. The churches that became involved faced the hostility of the police, fines and detention for some of the church leaders.

The price can be high for allowing the demands of Christ to shape our response to the realities of the situation around us.

Faced with the responsibility for cherishing the world and loving our neighbour, we deal with it in a variety of ways. We develop short sight and become busy tending to the problems of the 'neighbour'. Compassion and care fall short of God's best if they fail to tackle the causes of distress. Indeed, in this Christians may unconsciously play a part in maintaining an unjust social order. In our awareness of our own powerlessness to change structures, we may become long-sighted and see everything in abstract terms and avoid involvement at the local level. We run the risk of losing faith in God's capacity to transform us. We bristle if someone suggests that the issues of our corporate life are not optional extras for Christians to tackle if they wish. We want to be neutral, to shut our eyes, without seeing that to do so is to allow the present situation to roll on unchecked.

Christians have a responsibility to examine social organisation and structures in the light of God's values. There is an ever present need to assess how each of us is treated relative to each other and society and to see that justice is done. Throughout its pages the Bible reminds us of God's particular care to protect the weaker from the stronger. Our call is to co-operate with God in this.

A tall order or a high calling? In a way it is both because it is God's work that we are about. We want to deepen our spiritual lives so we pray as Jesus teaches us. We pray to see God's kingdom come and our prayer is more than words, it changes the way we live.

TAKE SEVEN DAYS . . .

Day 1

Praying is rather like looking in a mirror. It reveals a great deal about what concerns us and who we care about.

> Think about your own prayers and jot down the situations and people you are praying for.
> Listen to the intercessions in church, and later add them to your list.

What has taken up the most prayer? Is it something to do with you, the church, or the world?

• Meditate on Luke 1:46–55. This is a song of praise as Mary carries the coming Saviour within her. It gives a portrait of God's way of doing things. Imagine an incident in Jesus' life when he demonstrated one of the characteristics Mary describes in her song.

• 'Open our eyes, Lord, we want to see Jesus.' Ask Jesus to help you learn to stand in someone else's shoes.

Day 2

• Time is a gift from God. How are we spending it? Look at what you are doing this week.

How is your time divided up?
Who are you spending time with? Are they all Christians?

We need to give time to others if we are to be part of our local community.

• Meditate on Matthew 5:1–12. These are the 'upside-down' values of God's kingdom and are not a recipe for getting on in the world. Imagine yourself in the crowd.

Who is around you (see 4:24)?
What effect does it have on you to hear Jesus' words?

• Pray for those who have no choice about how they spend their time.

Day 3

• We rush about and often don't take time to see what is around us or to look for what God is doing in the world. Go and sit somewhere public: a library, municipal building, or street corner.

Be quiet and watch what is going on.
Listen to God, he is there.

• Meditate on Matthew 5:13–16 and 13:33. Salt, light and

193

yeast all have an effect. They change what they are in. What a waste if the light is under cover and the salt and leaven stay in their pots. How is your Christian community changing your neighbourhood?

• Pray for Christians at work. Concentrate on someone specific.

Day 4

• Make yourself a cup of tea or coffee! While you drink it, reflect on the fact that you are probably the last link in a chain of exploitation. Britain is the biggest tea importer in the world. Coffee is, in financial terms, the biggest crop in the world trade. Yet both tea and coffee pickers are usually paid low wages and live in overcrowded and unhealthy conditions.

Who do you buy your tea or coffee from? There are suppliers who make sure there is a fair deal for the plantation workers.

• Meditate on Amos 5:6–15,21–24. The stern voice of Amos reminds Israel that God will not tolerate injustice, nor will he be fooled by their religious practices. We will need God's help if we are to see injustice around us or further afield.

• Pray for the people working in tea and coffee plantations. Pray also that God will reveal ways in which we are contributing to injustice in this and other areas of life, and will help us to change.

Day 5

• Could you say what was happening in the news last week? When you read or hear a story in the news, take time to imagine what it feels like to be one of the central figures.

Try paying attention to items of news from one particular country, or to do with one issue. Follow that country or issue through for the next week or two.

• Meditate on Micah 4:1–5. God is interested in international relations. His desire is for peace. Imagine what it would be like if Micah's vision came true. Is it just impossible, or is there some step that you could take to contribute to peace?

• Pray for any local people, initiatives or groups seeking peace. If you don't know of one, try to find out if any such group exists in your area.

Day 6

• What is the most pressing problem in your local community? It might be to do with education, work, crime, housing, the environment.

Who is trying to do something about it?
How could Christians from your church, or you yourself, be involved?

• Meditate on Psalm 72. Here is a picture of a ruler after God's heart.

• Pray Psalm 72 for the leader of your country.

Day 7

• Political spirituality is about our corporate life. We are in this together. If you have been reading this book by yourself, find some other Christians to tell what you have been discovering.

• Meditate on Mark 10:17–27. It is frightening to think there might be things stopping us being fully part of God's kingdom. Let God show you what is holding you back.

What are the things in our lives, personally or nationally, which we think will give us security?
Can you believe that all things are possible with God?

• Pray for your church and its involvement with those, locally and internationally, who struggle for a more just society.

12

PRACTICAL SPIRITUALITY

John Pearce

If it is really true that at a particular point in time God himself, in the person of Jesus Christ, died for you and for me; if he loves the world (and you and me) so much that he suffered in our place and for us: then that incredible love must call forth a response. If we have experienced that very great love for us, then we shall want to respond by giving to God tokens of our love for him.

> Lavishness is the very law of his life. The Father is not just God, he is the source of Godhead, welling up, so to speak, in himself, but pouring itself out in the eternal generation of the Son . . .
>
> Meanness can never reflect God, and a mean heart will never come close to him. If we want to be with him, we must be prepared to live on the same scale that he enjoys. *Simon Tugwell*

Two of the ways we can do this are by fasting and by giving. Fasting is usually a private gift to God – something between us and him – and is to be offered to him secretly and with joy. Giving is a thank-offering to God – expressed in the form of practical love for our fellow men and women. Let us consider these two disciplines of the normal Christian life.

FASTING

Why fast?

In the modern world we are obsessed with diet. We are bombarded with books, courses and the latest schemes. It's big business. A lot of people will, for example, pay hundreds of pounds to go to a health farm for a supervised fast in order to obtain a healthier body. Christians may need to diet for physical reasons, but we should be fasting for spiritual reasons too. Fasting is a spiritual discipline which will move us on in our discipleship. The Bible also makes it perfectly plain that the children of God are expected to be people who fast.

> Strict exercise of self-control is an essential feature of the Christian's life. Such customs have only one purpose – to make the disciples more ready and cheerful to accomplish those things which God would have done ... When the flesh is satisfied it is hard to pray with cheerfulness or to devote oneself to a life of service which calls for much self renunciation.
>
> *Dietrich Bonhoeffer*

Jesus, in the Sermon on the Mount, spoke of giving, praying and fasting together: ' ... when you give to the needy ... when you pray ... when you fast ... ' (Matthew 6). While Jesus' words are not expressed as an explicit commandment, it is obvious that he took it for granted that his followers would give, would pray and would fast – and that what we needed was instruction as to how to do these things rightly. The New Testament references to fasting are only the tip of the iceberg as far as the Bible is concerned, and many more are to be found in the Old Testament.

In Joel (chapter 1) fasting is seen as a proper response to disaster, in this instance a disaster which is seen as a sign that God will be our judge. Fasting is a way to express our repentance – a way to show not only our sorrow for sin, but also our determination to turn back to God and to take him seriously. Joel called God's priests to give up not only food but also sleep in order to give more time to prayer (Joel 1:13).

The whole people (not just a selected few) were to be called to a solemn fast (v 14). In other words, fasting is not an exercise for the odd or the very holy but is for all God's people. It is worth noting that the fast which Joel called was a corporate one: the people were to fast together. While most fasting will usually be an individual matter (for which Jesus gives guidance in Matthew 6), there may also be times when the whole church should be called to a corporate fast.

Fasting, like any other practice, can be abused and degenerate into a religious show or pretence. In Isaiah 58 there is a serious message that fasting is not an excuse to forget social justice (vv 3–4). Our fasting must be the expression of a life which is lived in love, not only for God but for other people. Therefore, if we are to expect things to happen as a result of our fasting we must ensure that alongside the personal discipline there is also a responsible attitude toward our fellow men and women (vv 6–7). This passage can in no way be interpreted as an excuse to 'let us off the hook' of fasting, but as a call to a balanced spiritual life. And the key to that balance is to recognise that fasting is not just a utilitarian tool or a way of manipulating God. It is something which we can offer to God. It is a way of showing that he comes first in our lives and it rejoices his heart.

How does fasting help?
Those who have fasted regularly have discovered that there are four main reasons for fasting – in addition to the primary one of doing what Jesus plainly expected us to do.

1 It is a straightforward way of making an offering to God which is, in at least a small way, costly to us.

2 Fasting sets free more time for prayer. If we miss lunch, that makes available an extra hour in the week when we can give attention to God in worship or in intercession.

3 For many people it gives a sharpening of the mind and clearing of the will for a more concentrated and effective period of prayer. This clarity – the ability to see things more clearly as they really are – may not come at once.

It is usually associated with longer fasts or with shorter, regular fasts when practised for a long time.

4   Fasting loosens that which ties us too firmly to a fallen, self-centred world. We live in a consumer culture which conditions us to believe that 'more' is 'better', and will make us happy. Fasting helps us shake off those claims and demonstrate that it is obedience to God which brings true joy.

> It is not a matter of treating the body as an enemy and raining blows upon it, but rather as a friend whom one helps to play his part correctly. As many doctors say now-a-days, there is a hierarchy of the person, in which the body is not opposed to the spirit, but subjected to it, just as a good coachman holds the reins firmly, not in order to maltreat ... and paralyse [the horse], but in order to put it on its mettle and to guide it.   *Paul Tournier*

Practical guidelines

We need first to hear the words of Jesus (Matthew 6:16–18). Our fasting is to be without sadness or false solemnity, and is to be a matter between us and God. Jesus also says that 'your Father, who sees what is done in secret, will reward you' – a word which comes freshly to our ears.

It is of the greatest importance that we do only what the Lord requires of us, and not what works perfectly well for someone else but may not be right for us. Therefore there will be different patterns of fasting. The most common pattern is to give up a meal once a week, perhaps on Friday because it is the day when we remember the Lord's sacrifice for us upon the cross. The time saved from eating is spent in some form of prayer.

Others are able to fast for an entire day, although some people discover that, if they have a demanding day physically or intellectually, they need to have at least something at breakfast. A lunch time to lunch time fast – missing two

200

meals – may be a better pattern for such people.

Many people try to fast for three or four days a year at times like a retreat or during an extended time for prayer. Some find it necessary to eat a little – perhaps an apple or an orange. Remember always to drink plenty of water.

A few people are called to enter into a more extended period of fasting, perhaps for a week or two but, in any case, no one should ever fast for more than forty days. In most cases the fasting is offered to God as a prayer for a particular need, for example, for the conversion of a friend or for the removal of a particular 'log jam' in the life of a church, a business or the affairs of a nation. No one should enter on an extended fast without having had the experience of shorter fasts. And since the stomach and digestive system will have become used, during a long fast, to having little to do, it is vitally important to break a long fast gently – perhaps with a little fruit juice.

It is most important to take liquids during a fast, and it would be wise to consult a doctor before entering upon an extended period of fasting. There are certainly people who ought not to fast at all. Whatever we are called to do, Jesus makes it perfectly plain that fasting is to be done not with resignation but with joy and happiness. Fasting can be a new step in honouring, trusting and obeying God.

GIVING

Why do we give?
There is a fascinating story in 2 Samuel 24:18–25 telling how David built an altar to the Lord. God had instructed David through Gad, the prophet, to build the altar on the threshing floor belonging to Araunah the Jebusite. When David approached Araunah, he offered it quite freely as a gift to the king. However, in a moment of tremendous insight, David said, 'I will not sacrifice to the Lord my God burnt offerings that cost me nothing' (v 24). He bought the place and the oxen, and there made his sacrifice to the Lord. He could have said, 'Let Araunah provide the sacrifice', but David knew that he needed to offer a gift which would be costly to him;

and he did so. We need to remember David's example.

> When a friend of Alexander the Great had asked of
> him ten talents, he tendered to him fifty, and when
> reply was made that ten were sufficient, 'True,' said
> he, 'ten are sufficient for you to take, but not for me
> to give.'
> *Phillips Brooks*

Jesus himself expects us to give, although it is to be in secret
and without display (Matthew 6:1–4). Mark records the incident of the poor widow who gave 'a fraction of a penny' to
the work of the Lord (Mark 12:41–44) and he notes that
Jesus specifically drew his friends' attention to the incident
to show the great value of sacrificial giving. The widow had
'out of her poverty, put in everything – all she had to live
on.'

Jesus also endorsed the old practice of tithing. It is illumi-
nating to note that, in the process of criticising those who
are hypocrites in giving tithes but neglecting justice and mercy
(Matthew 23:23–24), he reinforced our responsibility to give
to God's work by saying, 'You should have practised the
latter [justice, mercy and faithfulness], without neglecting
the former [tithing].

During his time at Oxford, John Wesley began a
habit of giving which was to last all his life. For
example; when he was earning £30 a year and he
lived on £28, he gave £2 to the poor. The next
year he earned £60 and gave £32 away. The third
year he was able to give away £62, and the next year
£92. Much later on when he was earning, through
his writings, many thousands of pounds, he still
lived on £28 and gave the rest away.

However, we do not only give simply because God has told
us to do so. We are also aware that our giving may make a
tremendous difference to those in need. It will enable God's
work of evangelism to go forward. It will meet the needs of
the hungry and deprived across the world. It will set us free

from being too tied to our own possessions. For some of us, money and possessions can be 'idols' – and that problem needs sorting out before we can really serve God in a whole-hearted way.

How does giving help us?

It is obvious that our giving can help others, but how does it affect us? The clue is to be found in Matthew 6:19–21 when Jesus points out that our real motive for living will depend on where our real treasure is. If we live for money (or for our wife or husband, or for ambition, or whatever), that will in practice be our god. If we give of our money and possessions to the Lord, we shall not only be making a plain statement to ourselves of what is important to us, but taking a practical step towards dethroning false gods and serving God. If the setting aside of the tithe (or whatever gift it seems right to give) comes first, when we are paid, that may be an outward and visible sign that God comes first in our lives.

Practical guidelines

Clearly, what matters is that we should be serious about our giving and not allow it to be something which depends upon how much we have in our pocket or purse when we have opportunity to contribute, nor upon our emotional feeling at the time.

For many Christians the tithe has become the norm for their giving. Those who give sacrificially and are guided by God seem to cope, even if it may mean a much simpler lifestyle. And, of course, it makes life great fun! (You will need to decide whether you should tithe before or after tax – some social needs which we meet through taxes were met in biblical times through tithing. Taxpayers should be aware of the benefits of covenanting.)

However, remember that, whatever our pattern of giving may be, our level of giving does depend on what we have to start with. 10% of £80 a week is in fact a much more costly amount to give than 10% of £800 a week because, in the first case, so much less is left to live on. It is probably true that poorer people should give no more than one tenth (and, in some cases, less) and richer people ought to be giving much more, although all these things depend on circumstances, such as how many dependants are being cared for by the giver. The tithe should be seen not as a law but as a guideline.

In the end, the best guideline is Jesus' teaching: our giving should be secret and we need to remember the story of the widow's mite.

Other ways of giving
The principles which the Lord made clear about how we are to deal with money can be applied, and indeed should be applied, to the use of everything that is at our disposal. Our time and talents, for example, are to be used not only to make money and to keep our family and friends in reasonable comfort but also to forward the work of our local church and to help those in need. Once again, the principle of the tenth is one worth working out in practice. If most of us have, say, about forty hours a week which we can use as we choose, it could be right to set aside at least four hours a week for service of one kind or another. There is no space here to work these things out in detail: you will need to do that for yourself. Take time to think about your time. Take time to think about how you use your talents.

GETTING STARTED

These 'things to do' may help you get started on fasting and giving. Pray that God will help you to know which ideas to follow through.

- Record your diet for a week and think about it.

- Give away any possessions you have not used or looked at for twelve months.

- Fast from TV or leisure reading for a definite period.

- Collect information about hunger and poverty world-wide or in a particular area for which you have a special concern.

- Try to 'stand in the shoes' of the following people. You will need to collect some information about what life is like for them if you are to imagine something that bears at least a passing resemblance to the reality. Spend 20 minutes on each situation and try to think, imagine and feel your way into what it's like to be. . .

> A mother whose baby is dying because she cannot feed it.
> A homeless man settling down for sleep under the arches in London.
> A very rich businessman with homes in three continents and many possessions.
> A middle-class English Christian who has a comfortable income, but who doesn't tithe or fast and gives a few pounds a week to his church.

- Start fasting. Miss lunch one day and spend 30 minutes in prayer in a church or on a park bench.

   Plan a twenty-four hour fast of solid food. Plan to set aside three 30-minute periods: to read your daily Bible passage and meditate on it; to look at God or some aspect of his being, perhaps using a story from the Gospels; to intercede for specific people.

- Look at your weekly (or monthly) expenditure and income. What would ten per cent of your income be? What could you do with it?

AND THEN . . .

We have homed in on two parts of the Christian life, but each part of life is joined to other parts. We may find that just as Jesus spoke of giving, praying and fasting together, so we may experience renewal in prayer as we attend to giving and fasting. In the same chapter (Matthew 6) Jesus spoke of being devoted to God and seeking first his kingdom. Fasting and giving may seem mundane or restricting, but as we obey God in these things, who knows where our adventure with him may lead us?

TAKE SEVEN DAYS . . .

Day 1 In repentance

• Read Joel 1:1–14. A plague of locusts has been devastating the countryside. Hunger – indeed starvation – is in prospect. Whatever the farmers may do, there appears to be no hope. This disaster is a sign that the Day of the Lord, a day of judgement, is coming. The only response is repentance – turning back to the Lord. Verse 14 sums up the message. The whole nation is to repent and cry to the Lord in fasting.

• God will judge the world. Are we ready? Are our personal lives an offence to God? Do we need to turn back to him in fasting and in repentance?

• Make your own plans for a partial fast for three days. Try giving up something: snacks, lunch or supper. Perhaps you might change your diet to cut out luxury foods or limit your food to rice, lentils and vegetables. Or will you cut out all food for one day?

> How will you spend the money saved – or will you give it away? (If you give it away, what cause will you choose?)
> How will you spend the time saved? Will you give this time for worship, scripture reading or serious intercession?

Day 2 In sincerity

• Read Isaiah 58:1–9. Any kind of religious devotion can be insincere and only 'for show'. Sometimes we take refuge in worship as an escape from the real world.

Perhaps the way to turn back to God is to change our lives and, in particular, to learn to show love to other people by concrete action (vv 6–7).

- Pray: Lord help me to see beyond personal devotion to the call of the needy around me.

- What change is required of your life in order to obey verse 6? How far can you help the cause of justice? How much money can you give (as a result of fasting) to the needs of missionary work, relief agencies and those working for justice?

- Would it be right to fast from television and the newspapers for a week? This might mean less diagnosis of the ills of the world and more action to change them!

   How much do you spend on entertainment and information each week? Is it wisely spent?
   Do you need to study poverty and hunger and to find out more about it in preparation for some kind of practical action?

Day 3 In joy

- Read Matthew 6:16–18.

- Think:

   Fasting is to be a regular discipline.
   Fasting is to be done secretly and without parading it.
   Fasting is to be done with a face and demeanour full of joy and renewal.

- Pray: Lord, show me whether I should fast, when I should fast and how I should fast.

- Make a checklist of your food intake in a week.

   How much of it was needed and how much was unnecessary?
   Do you have possessions which are unnecessary and might be given away or sold for the help of others?
   Fasting involves doing something we do not, by nature, want to do. What could you do for God (or give away or give up for him) as a sign of your love and obedience?

Many of the activities suggested above are about helping others and loving our neighbours. But we need to remember that the first purpose of fasting is to show our love for God, to pray and to concentrate more fully on him. Read chapter nine of this book about Meditation and consider how fasting will enable you to meditate more effectively. Fasting can be part of making time for God.

Day 4 A costly offering

● Read 2 Samuel 24:18–25. David had a command from the Lord to build a place of worship for him, and a particular place was specified. David was determined to obey God's instructions precisely. Araunah, hearing the news, was anxious to give his property freely to David, but the king said, 'I will not sacrifice to the Lord my God burnt offerings that cost me nothing.'

● Consider how you can give to God a costly offering. Ask the Holy Spirit to show what he wants you to do.

● Do you tithe? (Is that before or after tax?) Is the tithe a minimum or a maximum?

> How do you dispose of the tithe? Is it still kept within your control or is it really given to others to dispose of?
>
> Does your giving go to the right places? What is a good balance between your local church, missionary work abroad and at home, development agencies, relief work, other charities and individuals you know who are in need?
>
> Is your giving planned, organised and prayed over?
>
> Do you have savings which might be used to make a 'costly offering'? Or do you have a duty to keep them to avoid being a burden to others?

Day 5 A secret offering

● Read Matthew 6:1–4. The New International Version of the Bible provides a sub-heading: 'Giving to the Needy'. Here

Jesus tells us how it is to be done.

What does this say to us?
Do we take seriously Jesus' concern for the needy?

• Pray: Lord, help me to do what you have commanded and show me how to do it.

• Is it right to give to travellers and street people? How often are they simply conning us? Yet there are many needy people on the streets of our cities. How can we give to them in a right and appropriate way?

What about all those needy people whom we never meet? How far do we need to make contact with them through others, such as ministers in inner city areas or rescue missions?

How can we avoid getting proud over gifts? How can we be secret in our giving? What, therefore, shall we do in practice?

Day 6 An appropriate offering

• Read Mark 12:41–44. Surely we need to hear exactly what Jesus himself said: 'She, out of her poverty, put in everything – all she had to live on.' Here is a challenge indeed! What is an appropriate offering for us to give? In one sense, our loving God draws from us a response which would give all we have. But, in practical terms, how much of our money should we give away? What is clear is that the ten per cent, for many people, is the minimum – although some people on lower incomes quite probably ought to give less.

• Pray: Lord, help me to be organised in my giving. Show me what I should do.

• Are you giving too much away? It is wrong and irresponsible to give away so much that you depend on others for essentials; but then, what are 'essentials'?

Are you giving away too little? Is your income such that it would enable you to give away far more than a little. What then should you do?

Why not make up a new personal budget with giving taking its proper place? And why not make up a 'budget' of how you spend your time. How much is given away? What about your talents? How are they used for God and for others?

Day 7 Self-giving

• Read Matthew 26:36–46. What Jesus must have felt at this point in his life! Because he was human, he will have wanted not to suffer what was, after all, possibly the most terrible death that men have ever devised. How did he feel?

• Does God call you to some sacrifice? What if he did? In what way does he challenge you now to a more disciplined, and perhaps sacrificial, life? Pray this through, taking plenty of time.

• Plan, in concrete terms, exactly what you will do.

13

TO BE A PILGRIM

Jane Keiller

The story is told of a small girl who, on her way out of the house, called to her mother that she was going outside, 'to play with God'. Her mother wasn't too sure what that involved and asked for an explanation. 'Oh,' came the reply, 'I throw my ball up in the air and he throws it back!'

Prayer is a two-way activity; to be engaged in prayer is to be occupied in a relationship. The individual pray-er brings to that relationship all that he is, his likes, dislikes, personality and character.

WHO AM I?

As you reach the end of this book, even a casual reflection on its contents will indicate preferences in prayer. Some chapters will have 'spoken' more clearly than others; some exercises will have been more helpful than others. This need be no cause for concern. The fact that one person finds being alone for any length of time a horrific prospect, and another finds groups overpowering, is no cause for guilt in the one who struggles to be silent, nor the other who battles with corporate prayer. God has made us for himself. The glorious truth of the incarnation is that he came to live like us. He understands us perfectly. He wants us to know and love him. So there must be a means of communication which is right for each individual. Although the purpose of a book like this is to enrich the prayer lives of all who read it, it is written in the knowledge that not every spiritual path is appropriate for everyone.

In our search for a personal prayer life there are times to look at ourselves, to discover our strengths as well as our weaknesses and to consider realistically who we are before God.

> One of the great tragedies during the past several centuries is that we have been more or less forced by training into a form of prayer or spirituality that was indeed a proper method for one particular temperament. Unfortunately that temperament belonged only to a small number of those who took seriously the need for prayer. One was given the impression that this traditional method of prayer was the best method for everyone. When it did not work, the conclusion was there was something wrong with the person rather than the method. Therefore, many of us decided that we were not destined for sanctity since the recommended way of spirituality could not be achieved, even with supreme and heroic effort. The result was that many good people gave up prayer altogether or went through the motions of praying without any real interior effect or benefit.
>
> *Chester P Michael and Marie C Norrisey*

Anyone whose answer to the question, 'Who am I?' includes being a child of God, is called to become increasingly like Jesus. This is bound to involve change, development and growth. It has been said of Moses that he spent forty years learning to be somebody, forty years learning to be nobody and forty years learning what God can do with a somebody who has learnt to be a nobody! God is in the business of transforming ordinary men and women 'into his likeness with ever-increasing glory' (2 Corinthians 3:18). We need to make sure that, as we grow, so our spiritual life grows; and to realise that what was appropriate when we were young in faith may no longer be so five, ten, fifty years on.

WHERE AM I?

> If you always pursue this determination to die rather
> than fail to reach the end of the road, the Lord may
> bring you through this life with a certain degree of
> thirst, but in the life which never ends He will give
> you great abundance to drink and you will have no
> fear of its failing you.   *Teresa of Avila*

The Bible provides us with a number of images depicting life
as a journey. Jesus described himself as 'the way', and he told
his followers to 'enter through the narrow gate . . . [for] small
is the gate and narrow the road that leads to life, and only a
few find it' (Matthew 7:13–14). The Old Testament records
many journeys: God taught Abraham, Jacob and Joseph
through their travels, and the wilderness wanderings of the
Israelites provided the opportunity for God to teach them
the basics of being his people.

Down the centuries, Christians have used this image of
life as a journey to help explain and describe God's leading
and guidance in the life of the individual believer. For Celtic
Christians, such as Patrick in Ireland, the idea of being a
perpetual pilgrim on the journey through life was central to
their faith. In his *Pilgrim's Progress*, John Bunyan popularised
the idea that Christians should see themselves as travellers.

It is not surprising that this picture has become such a
widely used description of the spiritual life. Travelling
involves the uphill slog and the mountain-top experience, the
drabness of the plain and the frustration of getting lost, all
of which find easy parallels in the Christian life. Journeys
also involve maps and routes, guides and directions, fellow
travellers and those who have trod the path before us.

The reluctance of Christians to ask for directions explains
why so many spend such a long time standing still. The
underlying assumption that we only seek help if we have 'a
problem' is a fundamental cause of countless impoverished
prayer lives. The fact that we will eventually reach our destination is all that keeps many Christians on a track which
they find unutterably dreary, when wise and sensitive advice
could bring renewed joy and vigour.

There is a time for sitting down by the wayside and looking at some of the alternatives available. Christ is, of course, the only way, but there are many *means* of coming to him and showing him our love.

WHERE HAVE I BEEN?

> We need memory to know who we are. We need memory to give ourselves a sense of where we have come from. Memory is the means of making the past consciously present.   *Oscar Wilde*

Throughout scripture God tells his people to remember their history. The rainbow, circumcision, the Passover, were all given that men and women might remember what God had done in the past and what he had promised them for the future. When Jesus told his disciples that he would send the Holy Spirit to them, he explained that one of the results would be improved memory: 'The Holy Spirit . . . will teach you all things and will remind you of everything I have said to you' (John 14:26).

However, even with the help of the Holy Spirit, it is all too easy for us to forget not only Jesus' teaching and his work in our lives but also our own failures and inability to grow in faith. An old lady once told me that the secret of her prayer life was her 'blessings book', a book in which she recorded the evidence of God's work in her life over the years. Not only did this provide a wonderful account of God's goodness to her, but its prod to her memory gave her a continual springboard for praise and thanksgiving.

The keeping of a spiritual diary or journal can be of great value in our walk with God. However, there are two main reasons which hinder Christians from such an exercise. The first is the time factor: it's hard enough to make time for prayer and Bible study, let alone writing. The second, more subtle reason, is a deep down rather vague belief that keeping a journal is self-indulgent, it hints at an over-preoccupation with one's problems and accomplishments – and such a pre-occupation would distract us from God and others.

On the other hand, the benefits of journal-keeping are

manifold. The very act of writing something down can be an aid to understanding. Times of difficulty and darkness can be lightened as we see traces of the hand of God at work in unexpected places. Times of decision making can be helped by the listing of pros and cons for the different courses of action open to us. Progress in the Christian life is often slow and a written record can act as a permanent reminder of where we have come from. A journal is the place where we can record our inner life, a collection of our personal 'God thoughts and experiences' to take with us on our journey.

TYPES OF JOURNAL

The pressure of time is a real one and not everyone is in a position to make daily entries. The following, however, are all legitimate alternatives.

• A daily record for a limited space of time such as a retreat or during Lent or Advent.

• A yearly record where one lays aside a space of time to write down one's reflections of the past twelve months.

• A journal written at significant moments.

None of these will be as effective (in terms of portraying an accurate picture of the ups and downs of the inner path) as a journal written on a regular daily or weekly basis. However, they will provide aids to memory and at least give the 'headlines' of our spiritual life.

A spiritual diary is essentially an intimate piece of writing. It is not intended for public consumption and this should help us to write exactly what we feel and think in the manner we wish to write it; spelling, punctuation and grammar are of no consequence. However, there is always the temptation to improve ourselves in the light of possible future publication! Perhaps the most effective check to our self-delusion and to putting a public face where we should be most private is to write always in the conscious presence of God. He knows our every thought and fantasy; it's not worth trying to pretend in his presence. If we are writing in order to know God and ourselves more thoroughly, then it pays to be honest and to record the bad as well as the good, the failures and the successes.

TIPS FOR JOURNALLING

• Don't wait for a 'significant date' to begin, such as the New Year or your birthday. It won't be easier to find the time to write then than it is now.

• Choose a book that is easy to manage. A commercially produced diary is not recommended as it assumes something will be written every day and the space available is limited. A notebook with a spiral spine is perhaps the easiest because it opens flat, but it can be rather too easy to tear pages out!

• Be realistic about your aims. Is it feasible to write every day? If not, don't feel bad if time passes without a word being written.

• Make sure each entry, however short, is dated.

• Be honest. For some people, the temptation is to paint oneself in a better light; others tend to do themselves down. Paul bids us to think of ourselves 'with sober judgment, in accordance with the measure of faith God has given [us]' (Romans 12:3).

• Re-read regularly, but *don't* revise.

WHAT SHALL I WRITE?

The fundamental rule of a spiritual journal is that anything can be included. Some people find it hard to get started. The exercises at the end of this chapter could provide a beginning. If you have already completed some of the exercises from the previous chapters of this book on separate pieces of paper, they can all be stuck in. If you haven't done them yet, you could have plenty of material to form your embryonic journal! Other possibilities include:

descriptions of events, people and situations
thoughts about events, relationships and situations
notes of helpful talks, sermons, Bible studies
quotations from books, hymns, poems, prayers
photographs, pictures, postcards, drawings, diagrams
snippets of conversation
newspaper and magazine cuttings
Bible verses
prayer requests
expressions of anger and anguish
outpourings of praise, psalms, songs
dreams, pictures, words from the Lord
book/record/tape/film titles you wish to remember
letters received or copies of those you have sent

It is your book. It is not written for anyone else; include anything which will help you better understand yourself and your relationship with God.

WHERE AM I GOING?

As we grow in faith, in knowledge of ourselves and of God, we discover that part of moving forward involves travelling deeper into ourselves. Teresa of Avila, in her teaching on the inner journey, used the image of a series of rooms or 'mansions' which make up the Christian's soul. The rooms are not in neat consecutive order, but Christ is in the central room and we move towards him as we progress in spiritual knowledge, and deal with those things within us which are not of God. The Christian knows the joy of having the presence of Christ in his heart, but most of us know only too well that there are other 'rooms' where the light of Christ has not shone and where the bogeys of guilt, regret, anger and fear still lurk.

If we could see beneath the surface of many a life, we would see that thousands of people within the Church are suffering spiritually from 'arrested development'; they never reach spirituality maturity; they never do all the good they were intended to do; and this is due to the fact that at some point in their lives they refused to go further; some act of self-sacrifice was required of them, and they felt they could not and would not make it; some habits had to be given up, some personal relation altered and renounced, and they refused to take the one step which would have opened up for them a new and vital development. They are 'stunted souls'.   *Olive Wyon*

Time spent in discovering who we really are (rather than who we would like to be) and in an honest appraisal of the journey thus far will help us to focus on where we are going. If eternity with God is our goal, then it soon becomes apparent that there are certain things we cannot take with us.

Fortunately God is preparing us for our destination with more determination than we can muster for ourselves. It is part of his gracious provision for our lives that he deals with our sin and heals our wounds. He doesn't want us to be 'stunted souls' and, if we will allow him, he wants to use us in bringing healing to others along the way.

WHO WILL SHOW ME THE WAY?

He who makes himself his own teacher becomes the pupil of a fool.   *Thomas Aquinas*

However much we can learn about ourselves from keeping a journal or by examining our responses to a variety of situations and stimuli, it is by talking with another human being that we truly come to know ourselves. Paul Tournier, the Swiss psychologist, has written: 'It is only by expressing [our] convictions to others that [we] become really conscious of them'. During recent years the value of finding another Christian who has more experience in the path of prayer and turning to them for directions has become far more widely recognised.

In the past, spiritual direction was seen to be largely a

Catholic activity. It carried with it connotations of authoritarianism and, as a result, many Protestants felt it was not for them. It was also, like journalling, thought to be somewhat self-indulgent, an activity for those of a spiritual disposition with plenty of spare time. Many have remained ignorant of the benefits of a director because they never considered the need.

What is 'spiritual direction'?

The task of a director is to listen. Human direction is based on the assumption that the only true director is God the Holy Spirit. It is not, however, always easy to recognise his guiding voice in our own lives. A wise director will be seeking to be a second pair of ears in the listening process and he or she will do this by their own prayer and by listening to the directee. The director's job is to ask questions in order to help the individual see for himself what God is doing in his life. It's rather like finding the end of a tangled ball of wool in order to unravel it and see how it holds together.

> ... I must tell the story if it is to become my story. In the telling of my experiences through the images and words related to those experiences I begin to own the experiences and allow them to shape me. In telling my story I appropriate the person I am becoming as a result of my story.
> *John Welch, O Carm*

Why a director?

A number of chapters in this book suggest aspects of the spiritual life which benefit from being undertaken with the direction of a wise guide. Fasting, the use of the imagination in prayer, meditation and discerning God's voice through his word – all increase their value in our lives if we have someone with whom we can discuss things both before and after embarking on each discipline. Our day-to-day pilgrimage can be greatly enhanced by having someone with whom we might reflect. Furthermore, there are times for all of us when it is extremely difficult to discern God's presence: unemployment, bereavement, a change of job or circumstances, often create an upheaval in our spiritual lives. Someone else can often enable us to hear what God is saying to us in and through those events.

Counselling or spiritual direction?
An individual goes to a counsellor because he has a problem. He goes to a director because he wants to grow spiritually. Visits to a counsellor are generally frequent and continue until the problem is resolved or dealt with. Visits to a director are usually infrequent and the relationship may last many years.

Finding a director
Martin Thornton, who wrote widely on the subject of direction, advised that one seek a director as one would a dentist when one moves to a new area. In other words, ask friends, or clergy, or anyone who might be able to advise. Local monasteries and convents can often be a rich source of directors. The value of the right spiritual director is incalculable, and seeking him or her should be a matter for serious prayer. If you make a few false starts, don't give up but keep persevering. However, remember that you are not looking for a best friend, although your director may one day become such. You are looking for a wise listener whose experience of life and of God you respect, someone whose advice you will value, but not someone who is going to tell you exactly what to do next. 'Competence is the only essential,' wrote Martin Thornton – so don't be too fussy!

Different kinds of direction

• Traditional one-to-one direction:

In this type of direction, an individual decides that he would like to talk with someone about his prayer life. Frequency of meeting will vary, but after an initial period of regular sessions (weekly or fortnightly) the relationship will usually settle into a pattern of two or three meetings per year.

• Congregational direction:

A growing number of churches are recognising the value of intensive direction for a short period of time for as many members of their congregation as can manage it. This usually involves inviting someone to be the church director for the space of a week. All those involved spend half an hour every day with the director. The knowledge that the time span is limited makes early morning and evening slots viable for those with full-time jobs.

• Group Direction:
This again is usually direction of limited duration. Its aim is to bring together individuals who are following a particular pattern of prayer, such as the exercises of St Ignatius. Prayer is undertaken individually, but participants meet together with a director once a week to share their experiences.

• Spiritual friendship:
This involves mutual direction and it can help two individuals to encourage one another, along the lines that 'two are better than one . . . If one falls down, his friend can help him up' (Ecclesiastes 4:9–10). However, in order for this to operate successfully, 'sessions' need to be worked out so that both parties have the chance to speak and to listen, and it should be understood that at some stage a third-party director can, perhaps should, be called upon.

TAKE SEVEN DAYS . . .

Day 1
• Meditate on 1 Corinthians 13:11–12.
There had been dramatic changes in Paul's life, not only the gradual maturity which comes with age, but drastic alterations in his view of himself and of God. Acts 9:1–6 and Philippians 3:4–9 may help in reflecting on Paul's transformation. Try to identify those areas of your life which still need to change before you 'see [God] face to face'.

• Find three or four old photographs of yourself, preferably including one when you were a baby and one as a child. Spend a few minutes thanking God for his love for you over the years.

How has he made himself known to you?
Can you identify any ways in which your view of God
    and your view of yourself has changed?

• Thank God for his maturing work in you. Ask him to
make known to you the areas for further growth.

Day 2

• Meditate on Psalm 23.

For David, who knew what it was to tend sheep, the
picture of God as his shepherd was an obvious image. Is this
a helpful idea for you? Or is there another picture which
would better reflect your experience of God?

• Where are you on your journey through life? Reflect on
some of the major decisions you have already taken.

Are there any you regret, any which you wouldn't change
    with hindsight?
Are there some paths which you would like to explore, a
    new method of prayer? A different hobby?
Is God calling you to a different place or job?

• Thank God for his guidance. Spend as long as you can in
silence, listening to God's voice concerning the journey ahead
of you.

Day 3

• Meditate on Deuteronomy 26:1–11.

God taught his people to use festivals as a special opportunity for remembering the goodness they had received. These
became the occasions when the children learnt their 'faith
history', and they enabled the people to say, 'Thank you' to
God in tangible ways.

For what would you like to give thanks?
Is there an 'offering' you can make to express your
    gratitude?

• Draw a horizontal straight line across a piece of paper.
This represents your life from the moment of birth until now.

Divide it up in whichever way will help you to remember the various stages. Look at your line and think of one person in each stage for whom you would like to give thanks.

• Thank God for those who have helped and been kind to you. Ask God to show you if there is anyone to whom you should express your thanks.

Day 4

• Meditate on Hebrews 12:1–3.
Sometimes we get lost because we lose sight of where we are going. The writer to the Hebrews urges us to fix our eyes on where we are going. (See also 1 Corinthians 9:24–27.)

> Are you sure that Jesus is the author and perfector of your faith?
> Have you 'grown weary' or 'lost heart'?
> Do you know why?

• Draw a circle. This represents the past twelve months. Now divide it up like a cake to symbolise the different activities which filled your time. The size of 'slice' will vary according to the amount of time allocated to each activity or relationship. You may find it helpful to leave twenty-four hours before pondering your completed 'cake'.
Would you like the next twelve months to be any different? If so, what do you need to do about it?

• Ask God to show you where you misuse your time. Is there a wrong attitude or relationship which you need to deal with?

Day 5

• Meditate on Acts 18:24–28.
Apollos wouldn't have had the advantages of the vast array of Christian literature available to us today. Priscilla and Aquila recognised that, although he had faith, there were gaps in his understanding. Look back to your exercise for Day 3. Amongst those who have helped you in some way, who encouraged you in your faith? Is there anyone you have helped spiritually?

• Is there a book, preferably one which you have read recently, which has been particularly helpful or inspiring to your faith? Think of someone to whom you could lend it.

• Do you have someone with whom you can talk about your faith? If so, thank God for them; if not, ask that God might guide you to someone.

Day 6

• Meditate on Mark 10:46–52.
  Bartimaeus could only sit by the wayside and call for help. Imagine yourself in his place. Think of what he might have heard, felt and smelt as he sat by the roadside. What would it feel like to have his past, to have his future (or lack of it)? Feel his despair and isolation. Hear yourself shouting and then, miraculously, being called. Jesus is beside you asking, 'What do you want me to do for you?' What is your reply?

• Jesus said, 'Even the very hairs of your head are all numbered' (Matthew 10:30). Run your hands through your hair a few times.

> What does it mean to you to know that God knows you that well?
> Does your prayer life reflect God's intimate knowledge and love for you?

• Ask God to help you respond to his infinite love.

Day 7

• Meditate on Psalm 25:4–12.
  David could look back over his life and see God's forgiveness, guidance and love. What has God been teaching you through the past week's exercises?

• Make a list of as many scripture verses as you can remember which have 'spoken' to you in the past.

> Can you see any pattern in the way God has guided you?
> Do any of these verses speak to your present situation?

• Use Psalm 25:4–12 as a prayer.